WITHDRAWN

INCREDIBLE 3D STEREOGRAMS

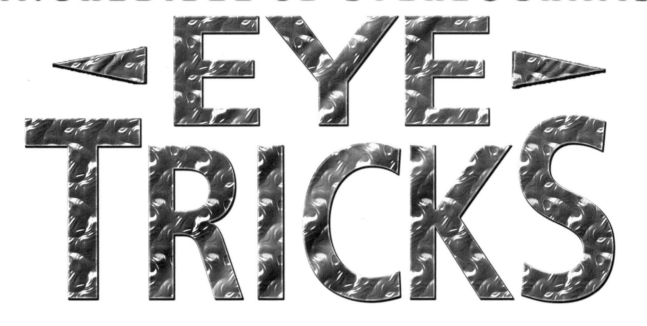

EYE TRICKS

Gary W. Priester and Gene Levine

CHARTWELL
BOOKS, INC.

Gary W. Priester lives in Placitas, New Mexico USA and can be contacted via e-mail at gary@gwpriester.com. To see additional works created by Gary, please visit http://www.gwpriester.com.

Gene Levine lives in Los Angeles, California USA and can be contacted via e-mail at gene_levine@colorstereo.com. To see additional works created by Gene, please visit http://www.colorstereo.com.

This book was created in association with eyetricks.com. For more information visit http://www.eyetricks.com.

eyetricks.com

This edition printed in 2005 by
CHARTWELL BOOKS, INC.
A Division of
BOOK SALES, INC.
114 Northfield Avenue
Edison, New Jersey 08837

Copyright © 2004 Arcturus Publishing Limited
26/27 Bickels Yard, 151–153 Bermondsey Street,
London SE1 3HA

ISBN-13: 978-0-7858-2055-0
ISBN-10: 0-7858-2055-8

Printed in China

Author accreditation
Images on pages 8-26, 28-59, 110, 140-143, 165-169, 172-179, 182-187, 189-207 were designed and created by Gene Levine. Images on pages 27, 60-109, 111-139, 144-164, 170-171, 180-181 and 188 are the design and creation of Gary W. Priester.

Contents

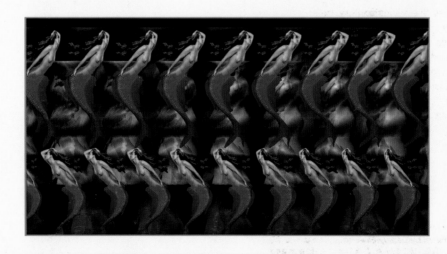

How to view stereograms

This is intended as a guide for viewers who have never seen stereogram 3D effects, and for those viewers who are a bit rusty. Please don't be discouraged if you can't visualize the effects right away. After all, what you are doing is overcoming a lifetime habit of viewing everything with 'normal' stereovision: that which gives us a sense of depth in our everyday viewing of the world.

First, let's try using a physical aid. After that are some practices for viewing autostereograms (stereograms that work without physical aids).

To view hidden-image and stereo-field stereograms, you cannot use normal, or cross-eyed vision (see fig. 1). Instead, you have to use parallel vision, which is what you will do automatically if you place a piece of card between your eyes when viewing the images (see fig. 2).

Unlike cross-eyed vision, there is no strain or discomfort with parallel vision. The essential key, in fact, is to relax your eyes into viewing this way.

Below is a stereo-pair image. Place the card directly in the middle of the pair, as illustrated in fig. 2. Now move your head to position the other end of the card between your eyes. Disregard focusing for now.

A stereo-pair

If the alignment is good, you should see only one image. Now relax your eyes, and slowly bring things into focus, pulling your head back. Remember, you should not think you see a 3D effect; you should know for sure. When you are sure, hold that focus and remove the card. You should now see three images: the one in the middle containing the 3D effects.

Congratulations, you are now viewing a stereogram as it should be seen!

Continue with the practices without aids, opposite. The only thing you'll need here is two eyes. Let go of the normal way you focus on something on a page. Let your eyes relax.

fig. 1 **Normal vision**   fig. 2 **Parallel vision**

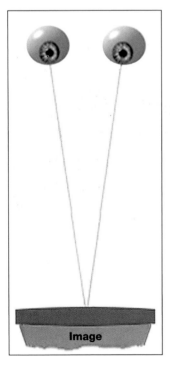
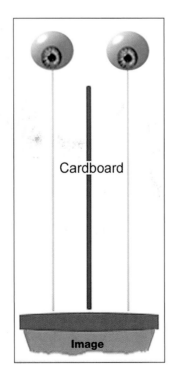

Cardboard

Image   Image

Top view

Viewing practice for autostereograms

Practice 1

The objective here is to let your mind process these two objects until they appear as three. Let your eyes relax, and move your head forward or away until three zeros appear clearly.

Your primary inclination is to focus on the above two objects in the normal way. But now, look behind them; look behind the page and forget about focusing. Try this for a while until you gradually see the three zeros.

When you see a non-existent object appear between the two existing ones, you have mastered the basis of the stereo-pair. It is in the centre object where the 3D effect takes place. This is the crux of autostereograms.

So where does the centre image come from?

It is helpful to remember that visual perception happens in the brain, not the eyes. What we're doing here is fooling the brain. The eyes are feeding it visual information, but not in the usual manner, and so the mind gives us a middle object. And if you introduce some subtle offsets and distortions into two otherwise similar images, the mind will perceive depth even though it is not truly there.

If you view three objects as an autostereogram, you should perceive four objects. Four objects will look as if they are five, and so on.

Practice 2

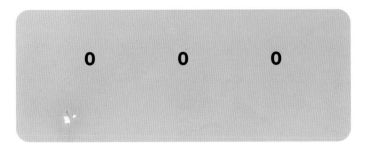

And now for some 3D:

Between these two objects, another object should appear with the smaller square floating over the larger.

Practice 3

Still can't see it?

Pull back, and focus normally on the centre object of the three below. Now lean slowly forward into the page, holding that focus until it is broken or you see four objects, clearly.

Master these practices, and you should have no problem moving on to fully-fledged autostereograms.

Practice 4

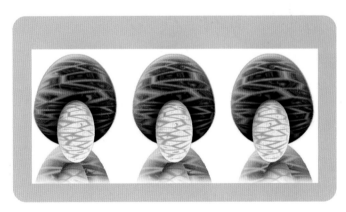

view this way

© 2004
GENE LEVI

© 2002 GENE LEVINE

view this way

view this way

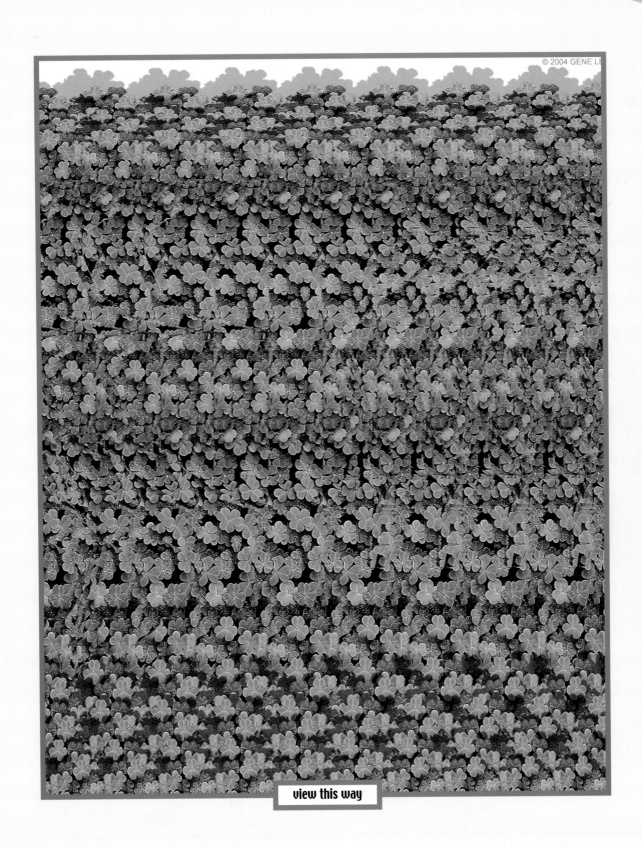

view this way

Blossom Waves

view this way

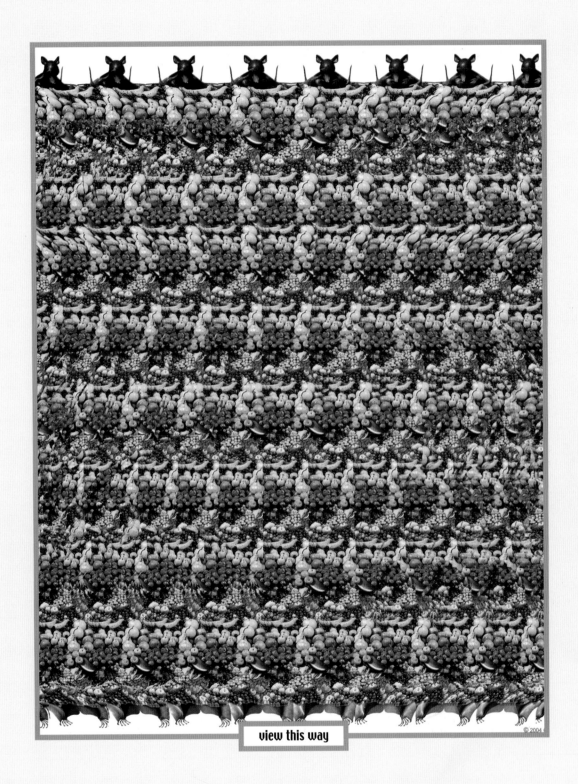

view this way

© 2004

Cherry Blossom

view this way

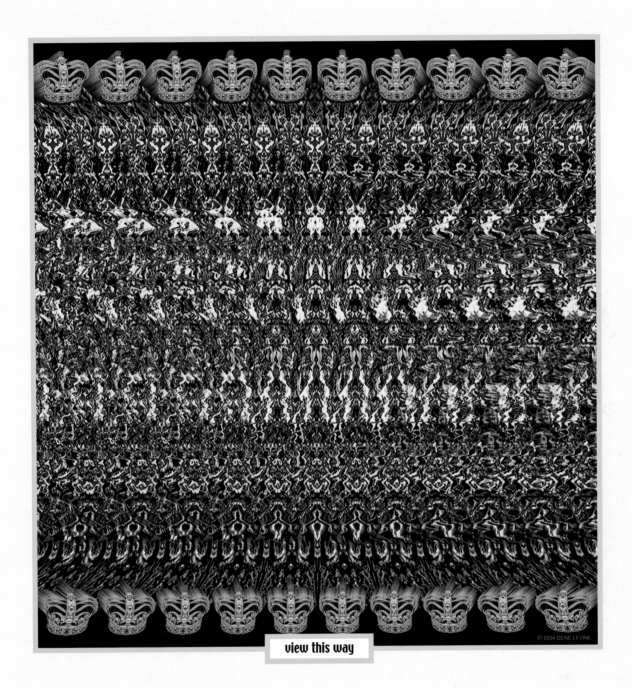

view this way

© 2004 GENE LEVINE

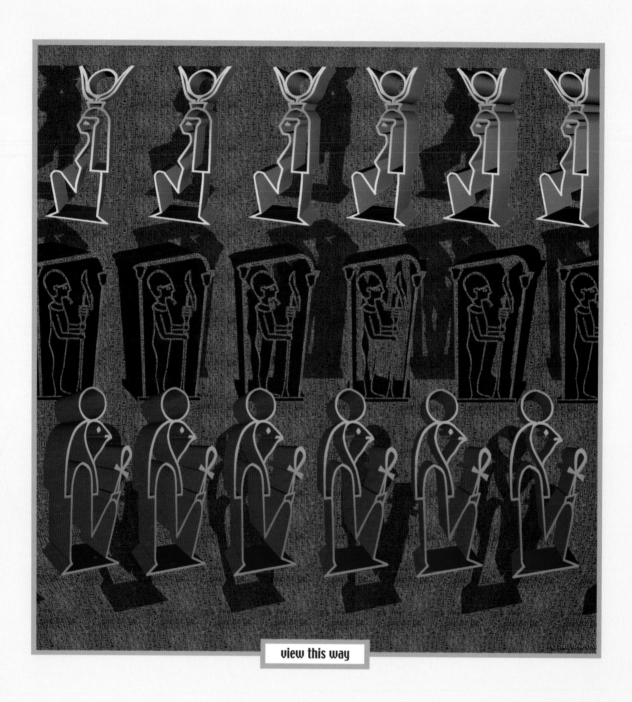

view this way

© 2002 GENE LEVINE

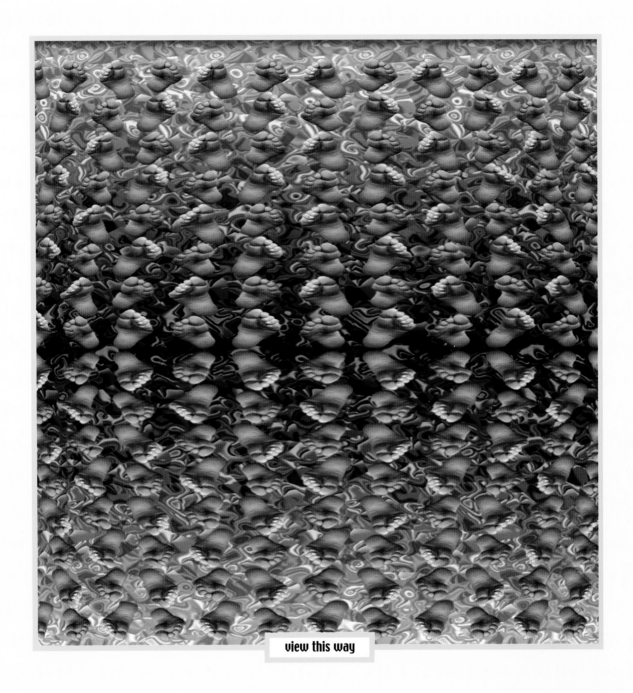

view this way

Stereocycle

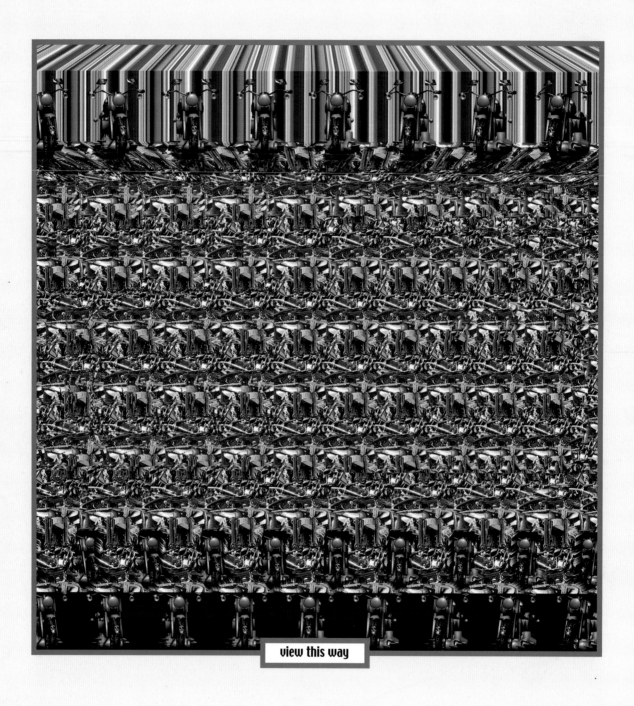

view this way

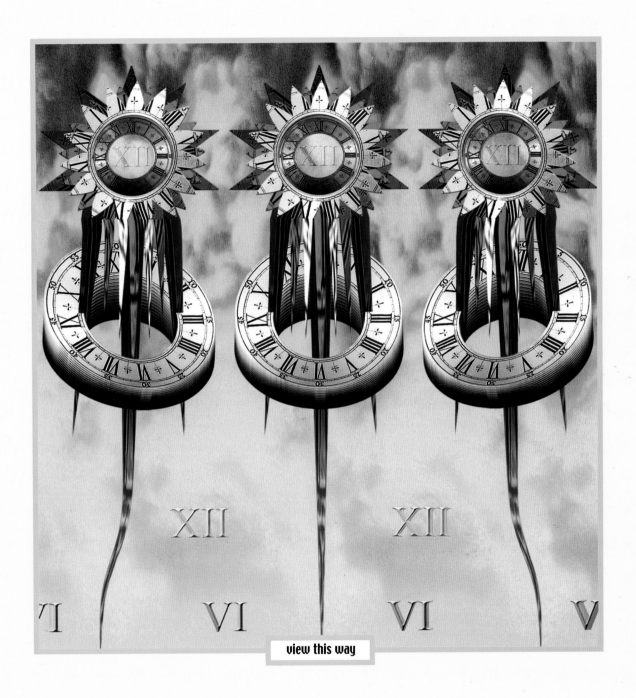

view this way

Lake View

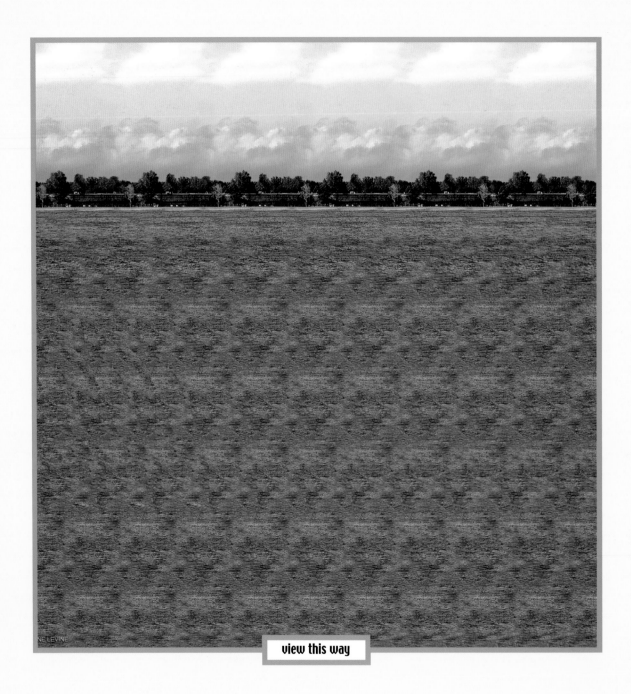

view this way

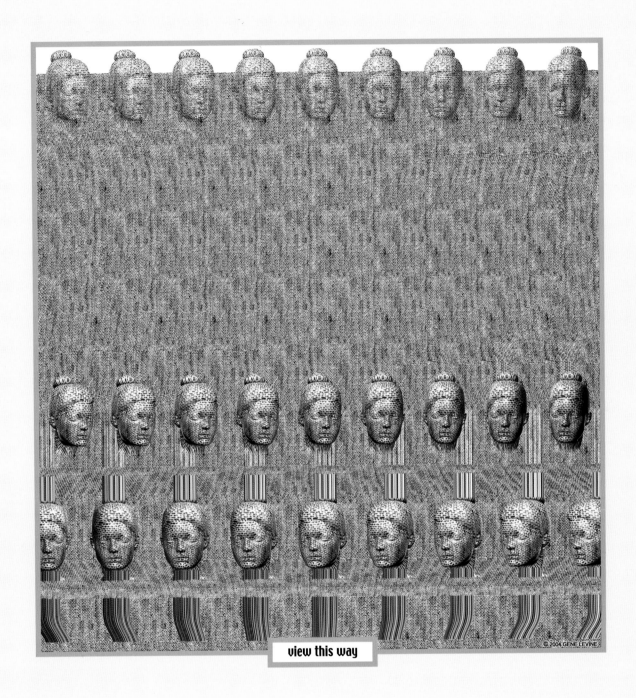

view this way

© 2004 GENE LEVINE

Wing Wang

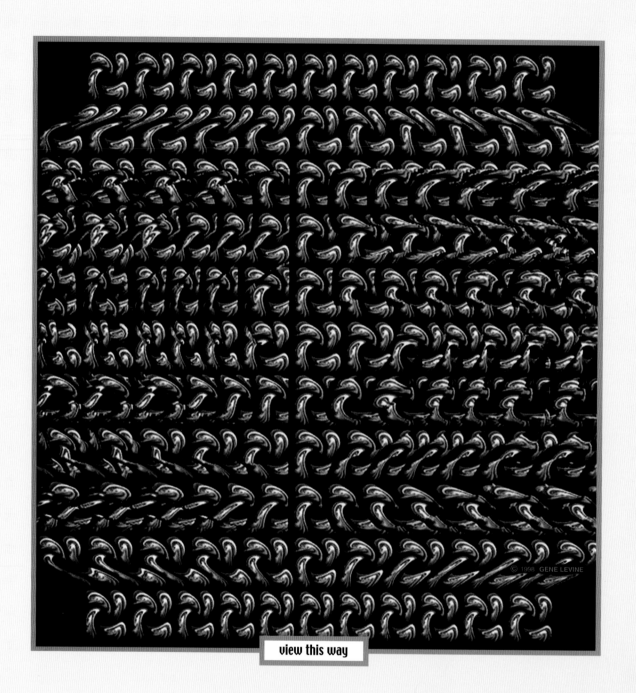

view this way

22

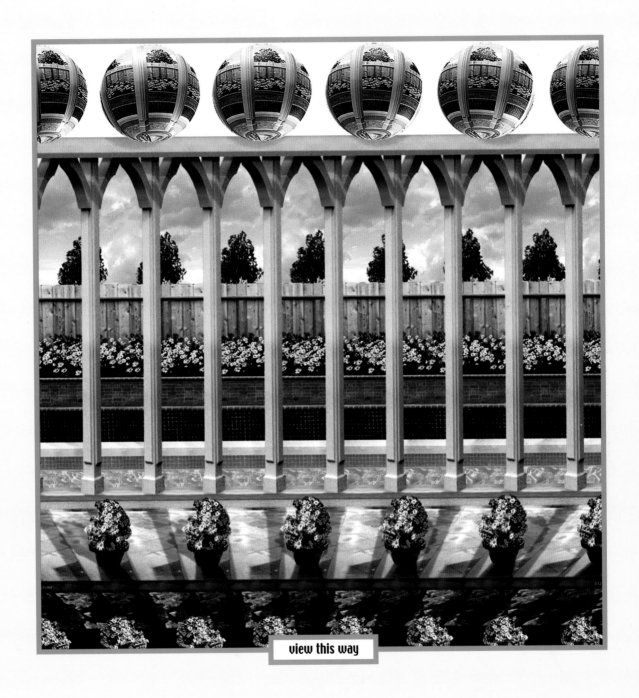

view this way

King & Queen

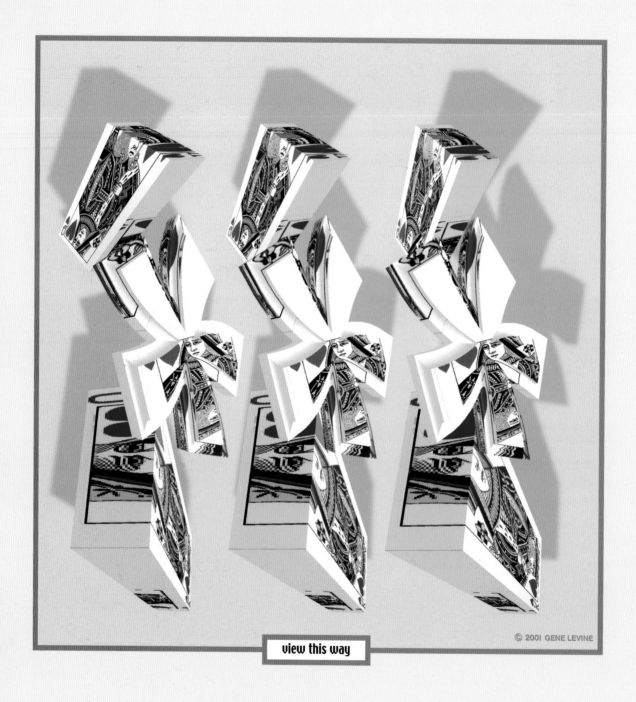

view this way

© 2001 GENE LEVINE

24

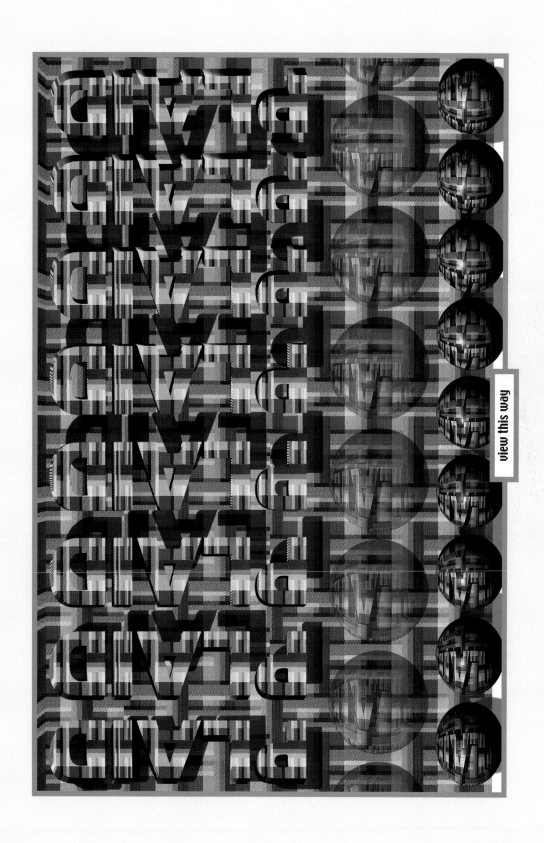

view this way

Point Burst

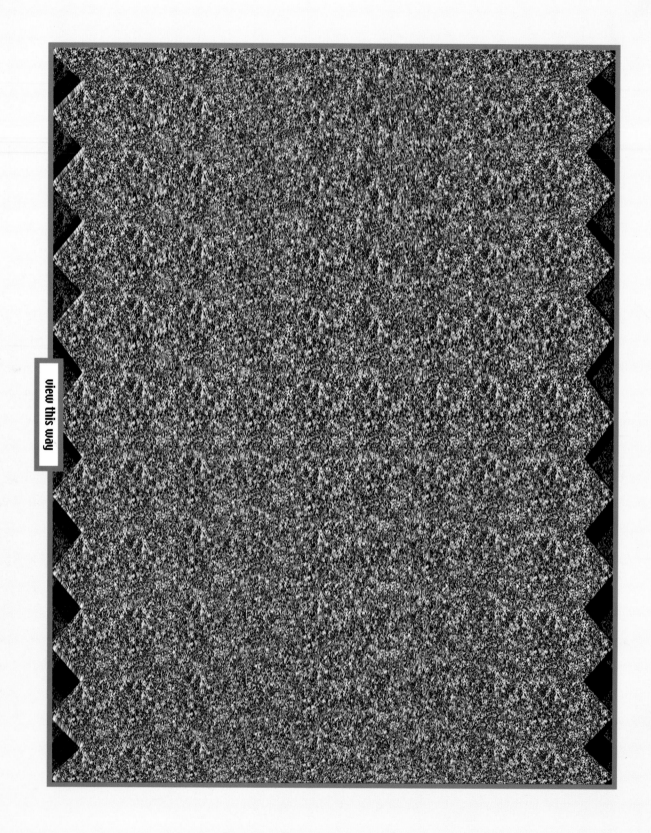

view this way

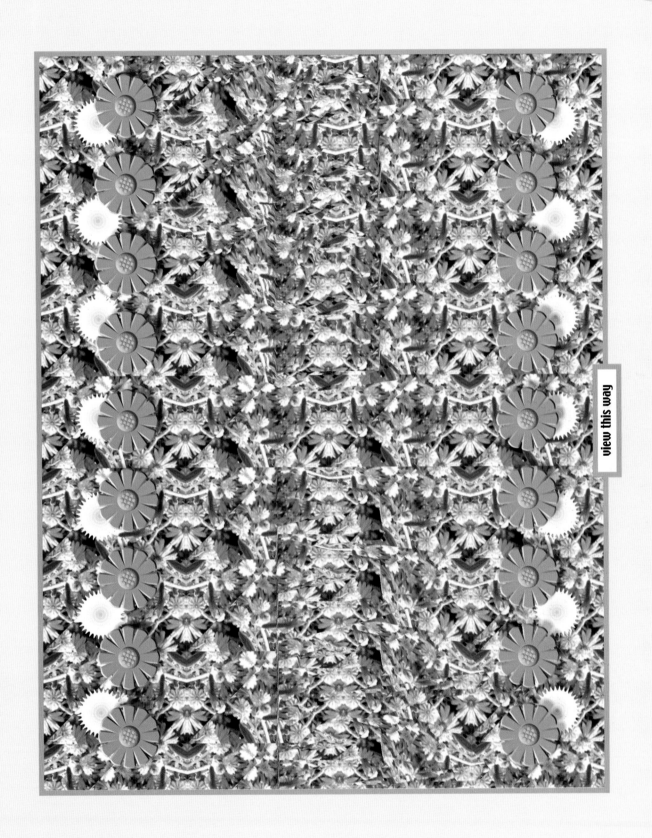

view this way

Diamonds in the Rough

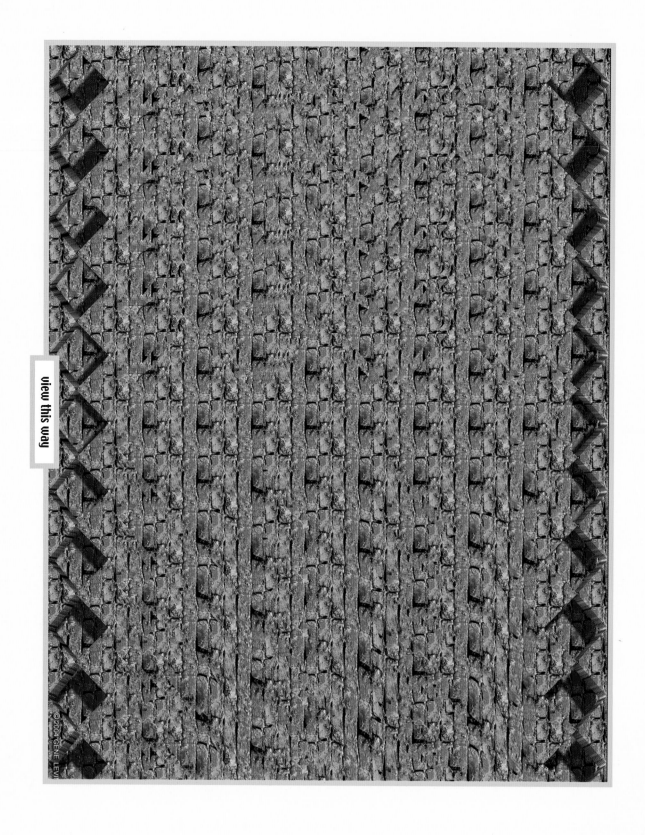

view this way

© 2004 GENE LEVI

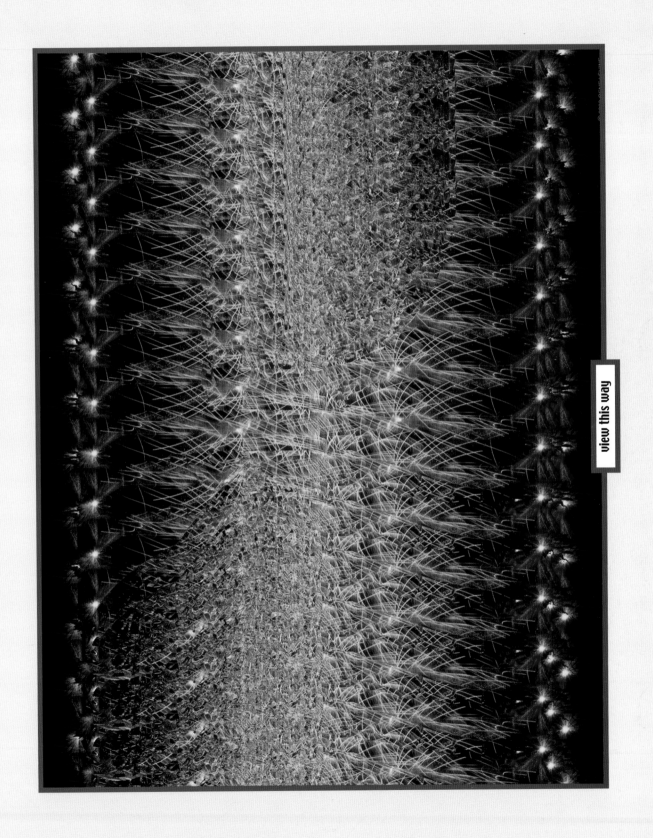

view this way

view this way

© 2003 GENE LEVINE

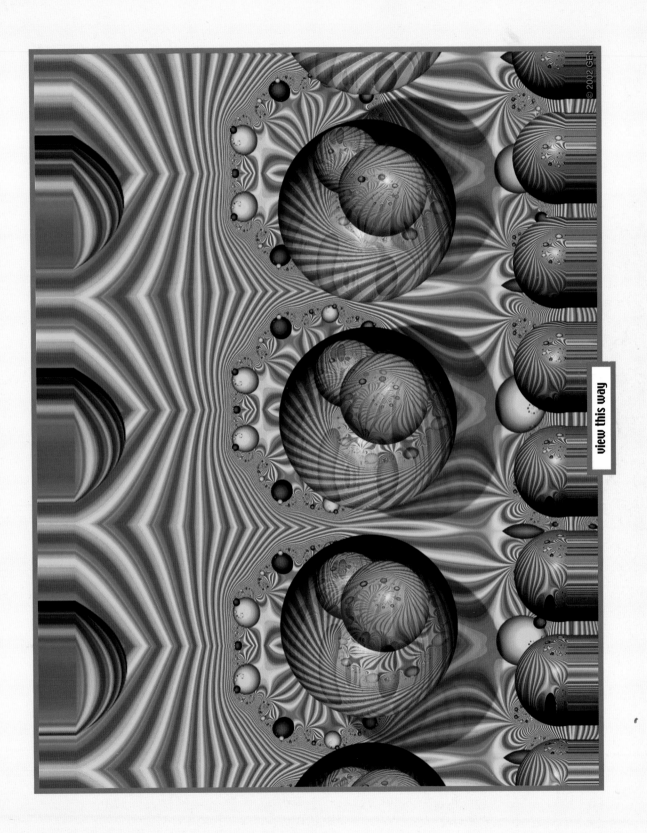

view this way

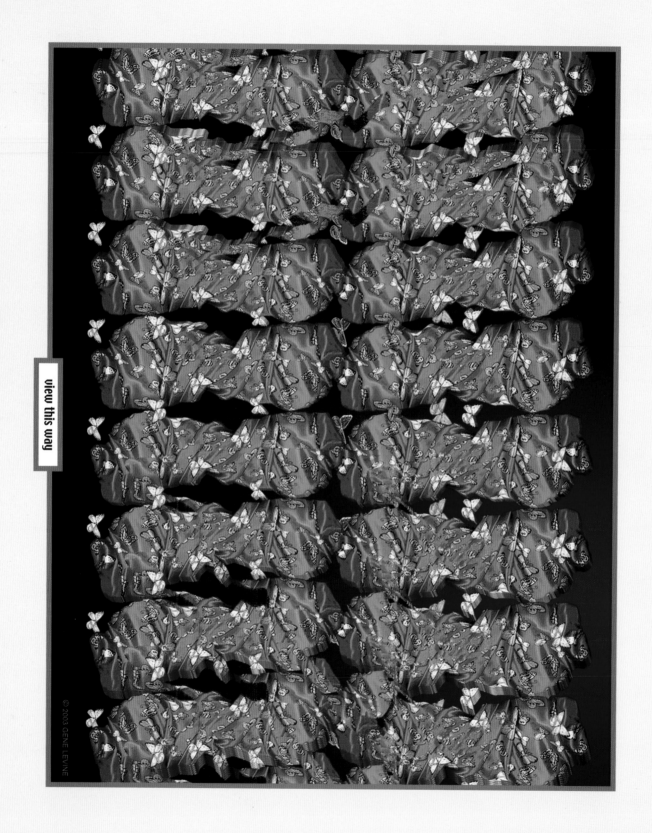

view this way

© 2003 GENE LEVINE

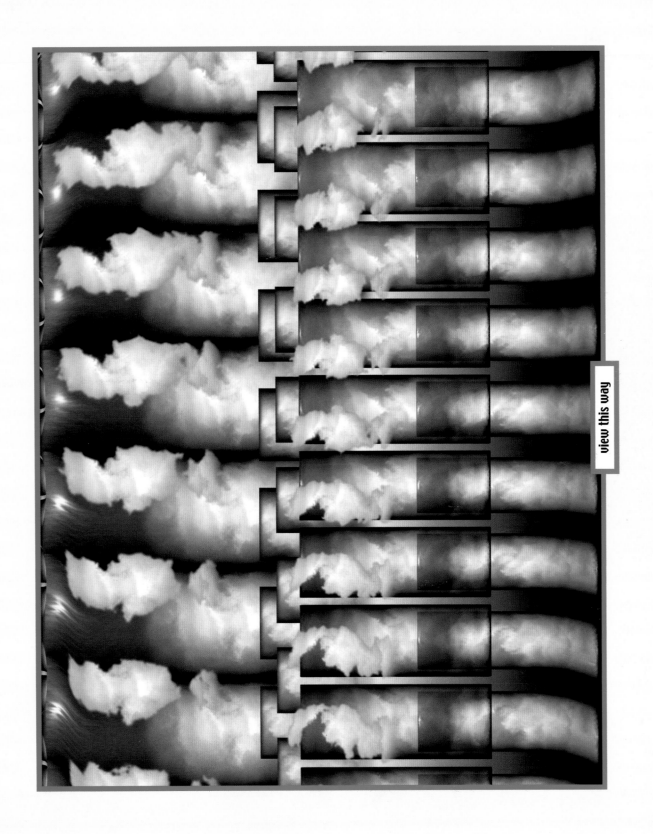

view this way

Colour Sieve

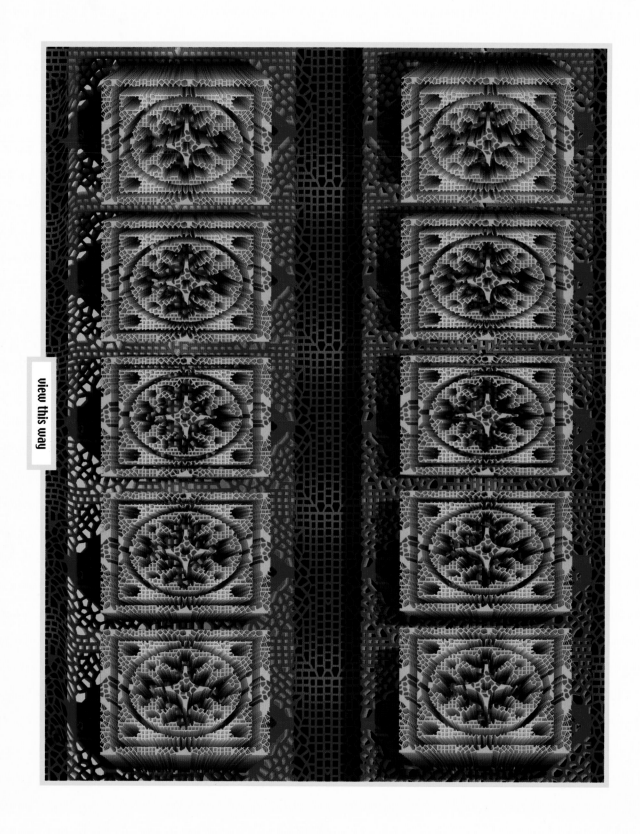

view this way

view this way

Molten Water

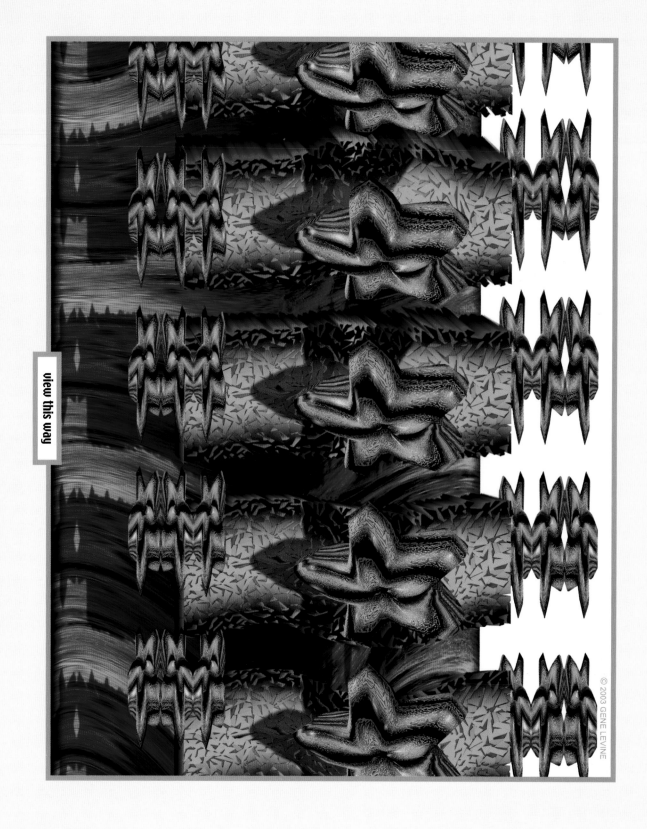

view this way

view this way

Star Screen

view this way

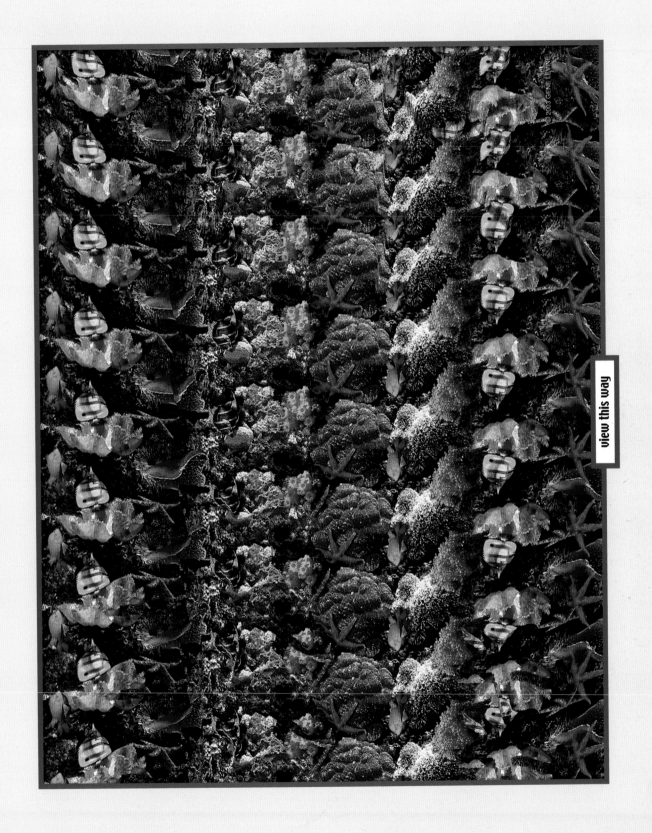

© 2003 GENE LEVINE

view this way

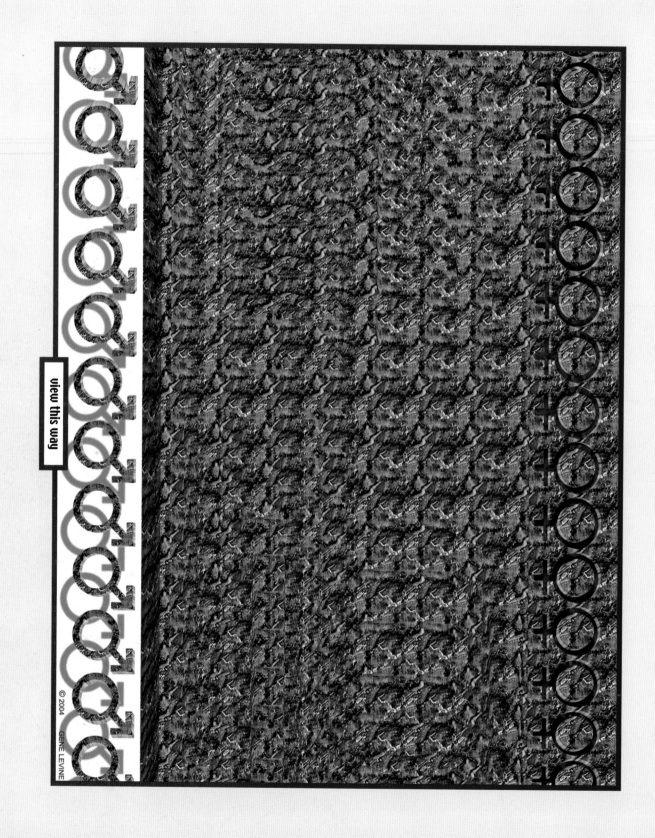

view this way

© 2004 GENE LEVINE

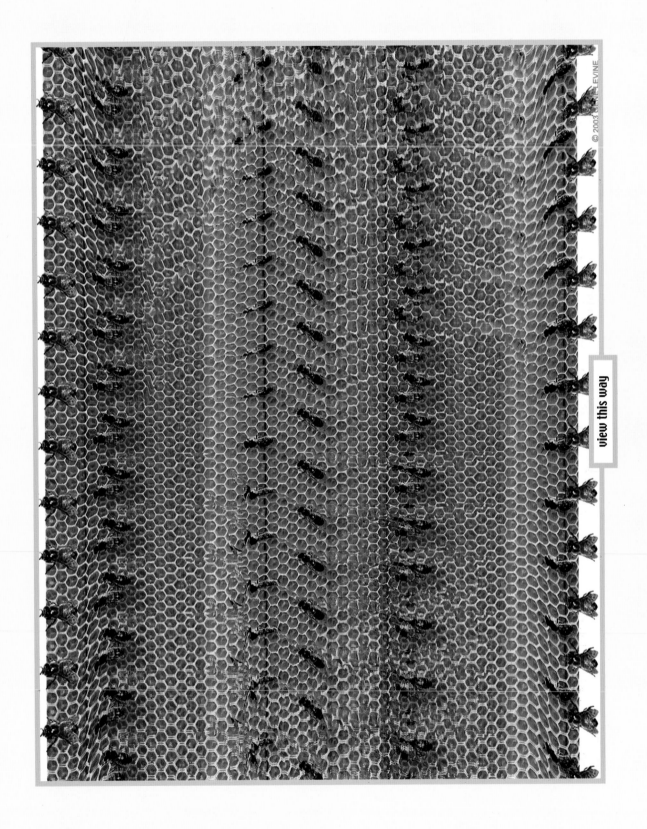

view this way

Hidden Image

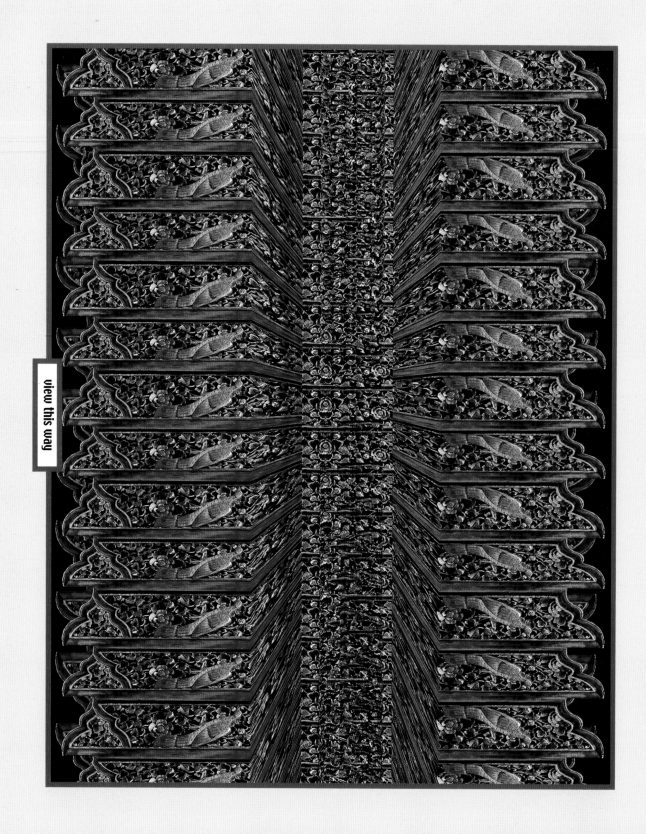

view this way

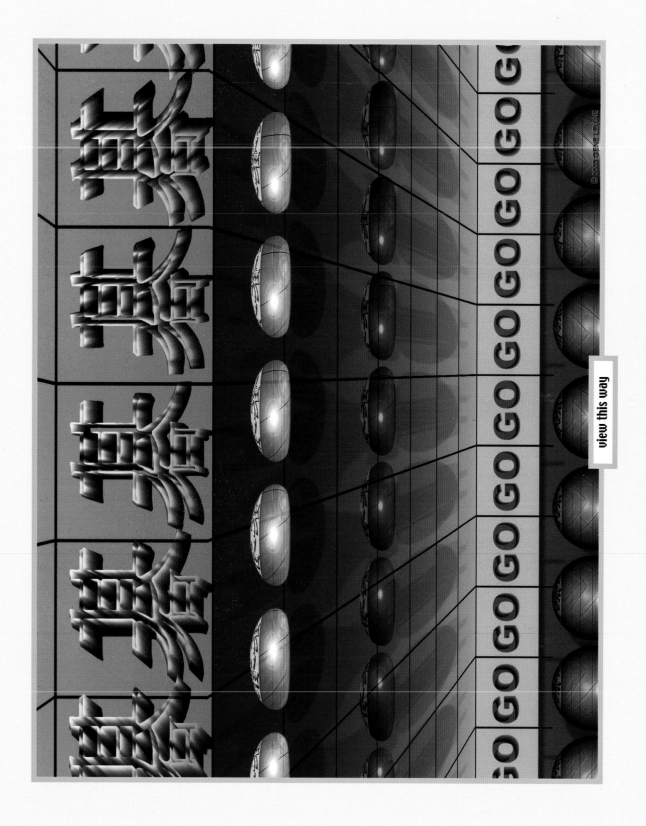

view this way

Fireworks

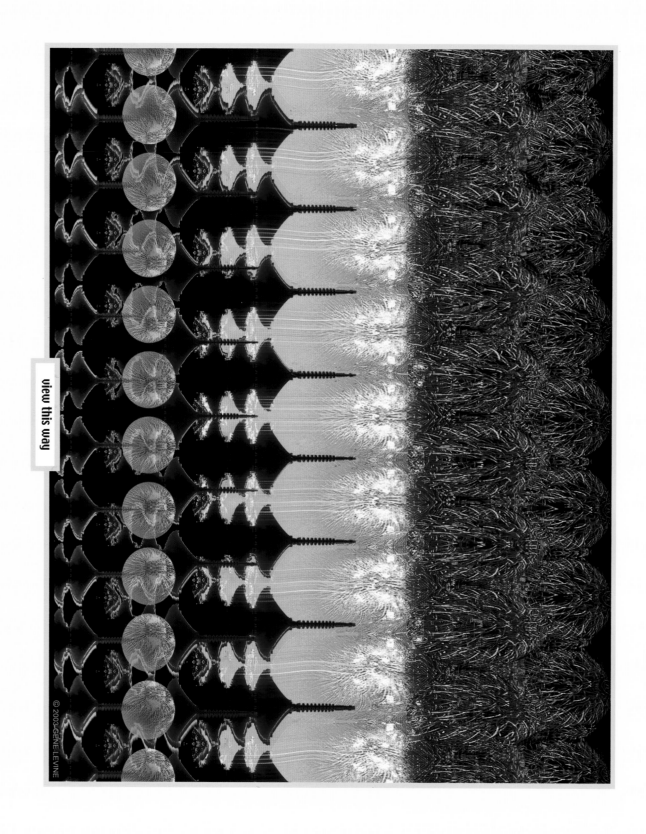

view this way

© 2003 GENE LEVINE

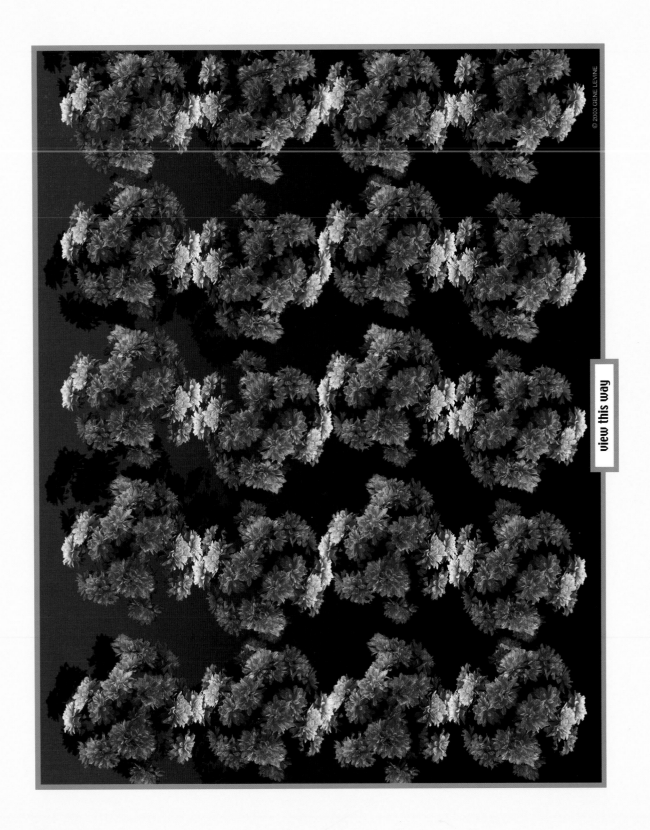

© 2003 GENE LEVINE

view this way

Footprints

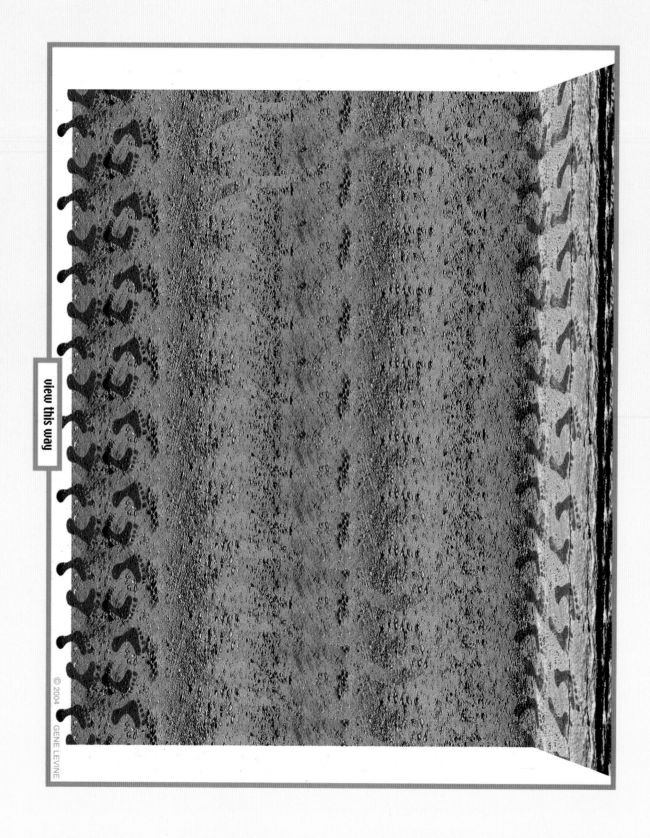

view this way

© 2004 GENE LEVINE

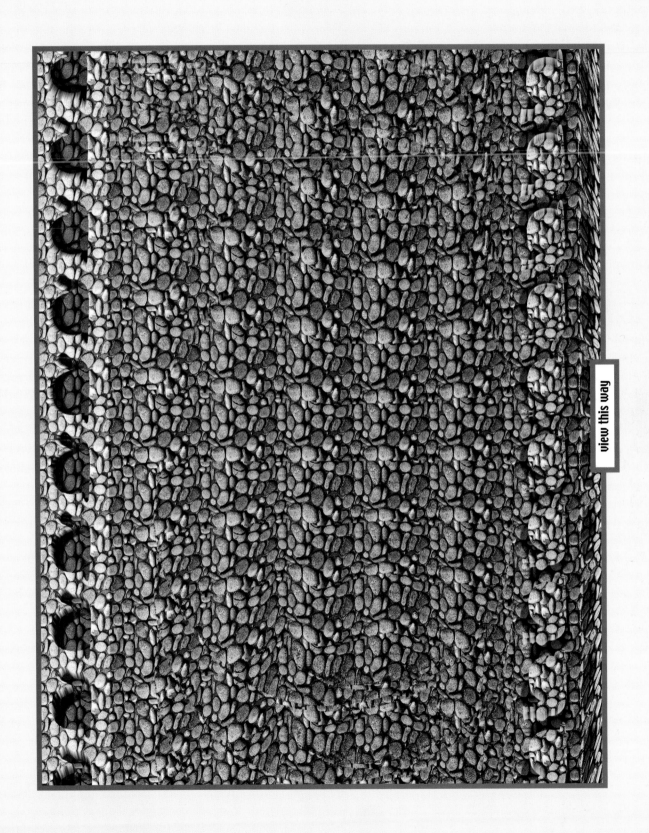

view this way

view this way

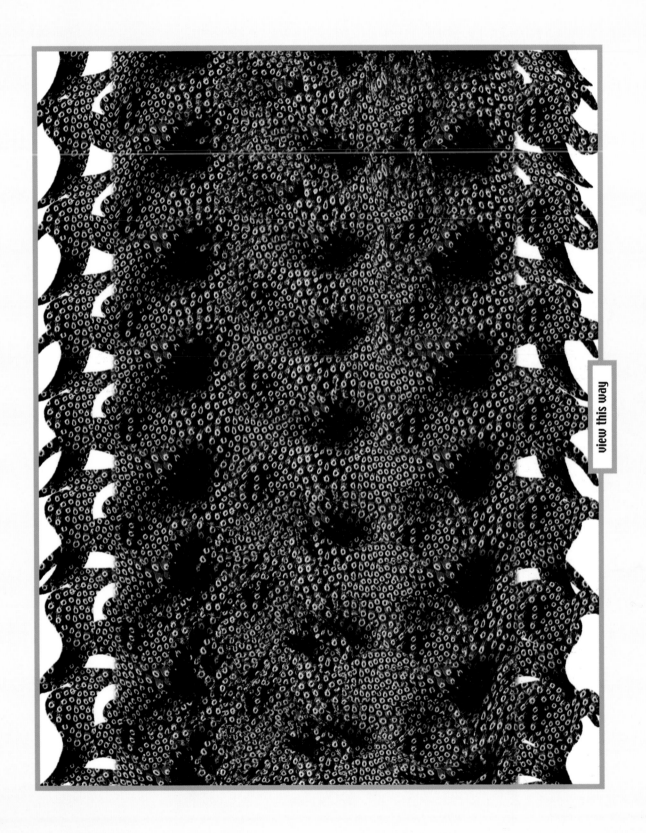

view this way

Stone Burst

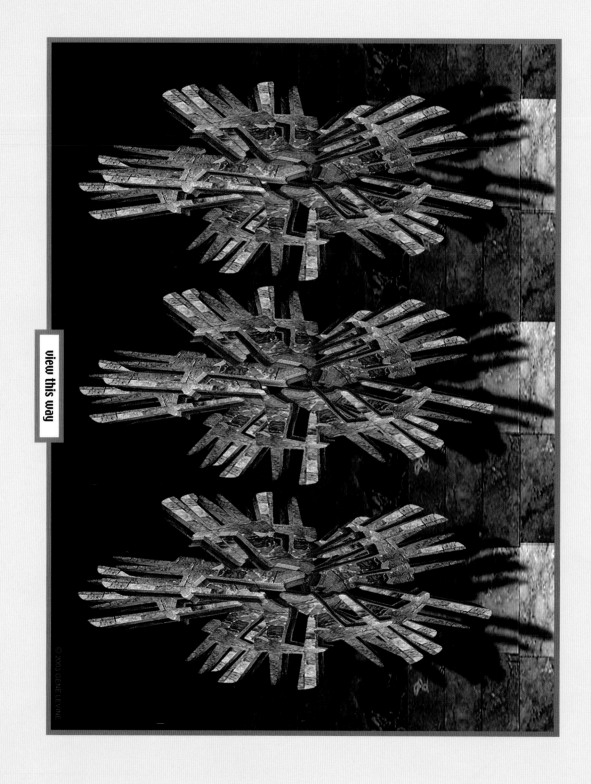

view this way

© 2003 GENE LEVINE

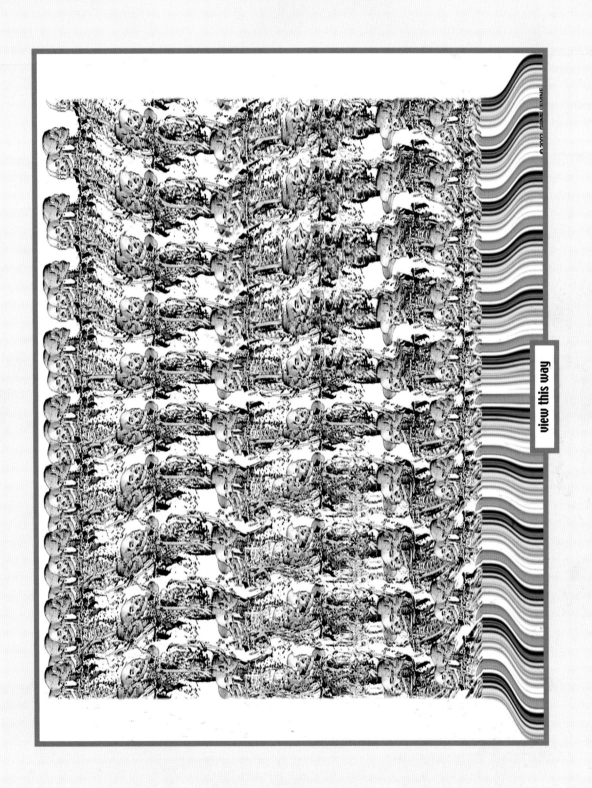

view this way

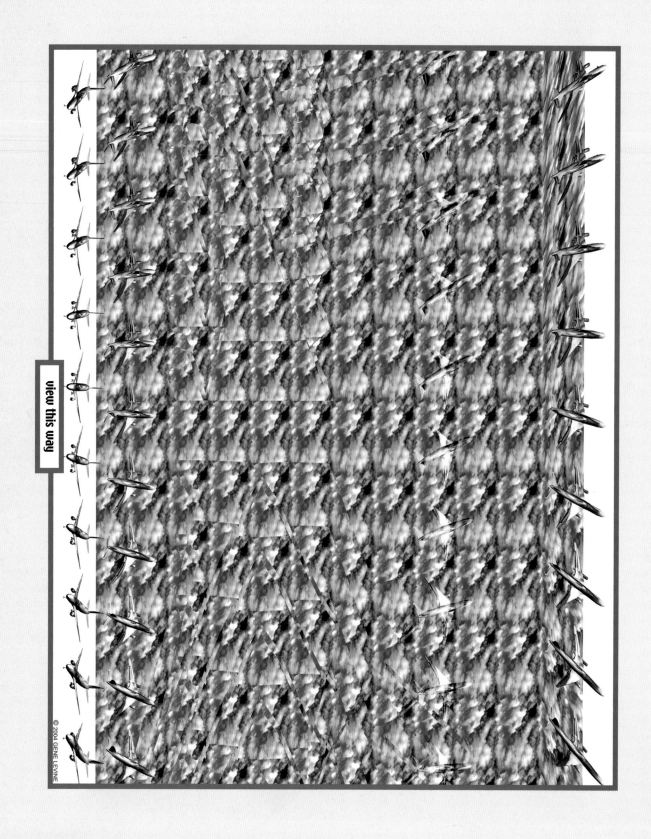

view this way

© 2004 GENE LEVINE

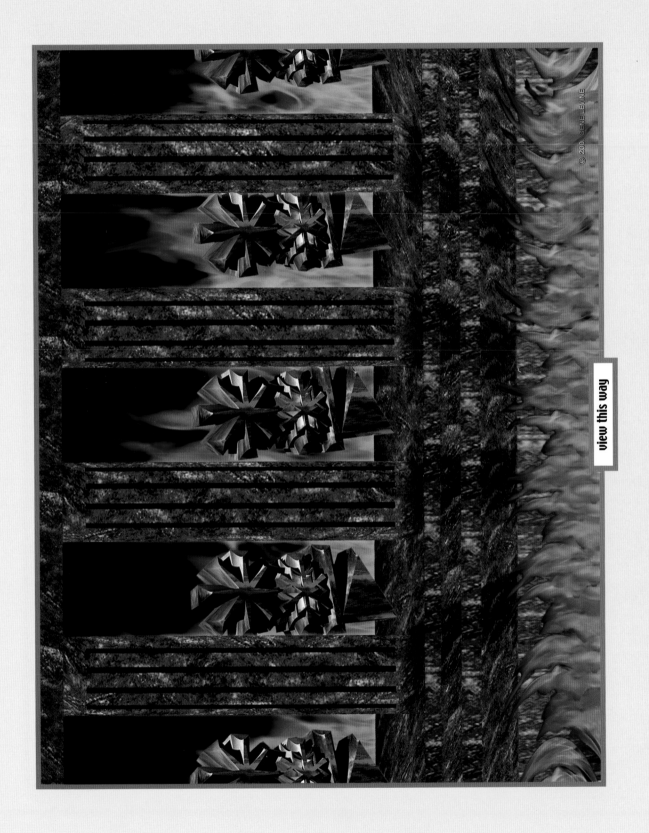

Heart in Heart

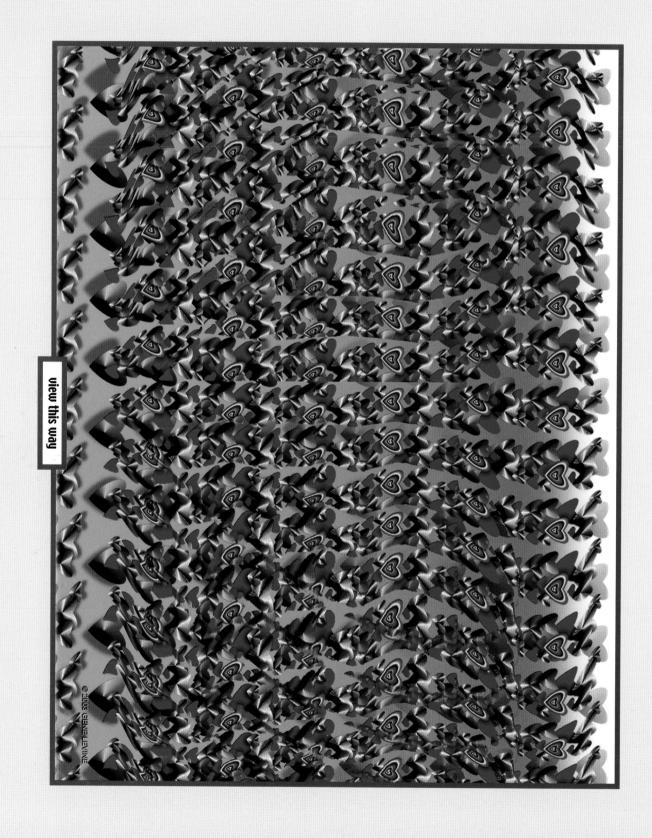

view this way

© 2003 GENE LEVINE

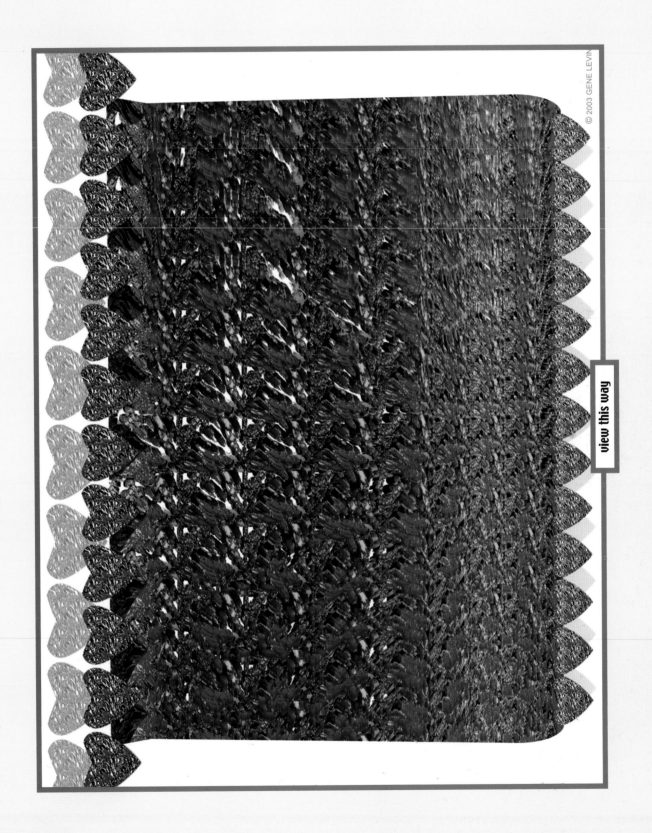

view this way

Terraced

view this way

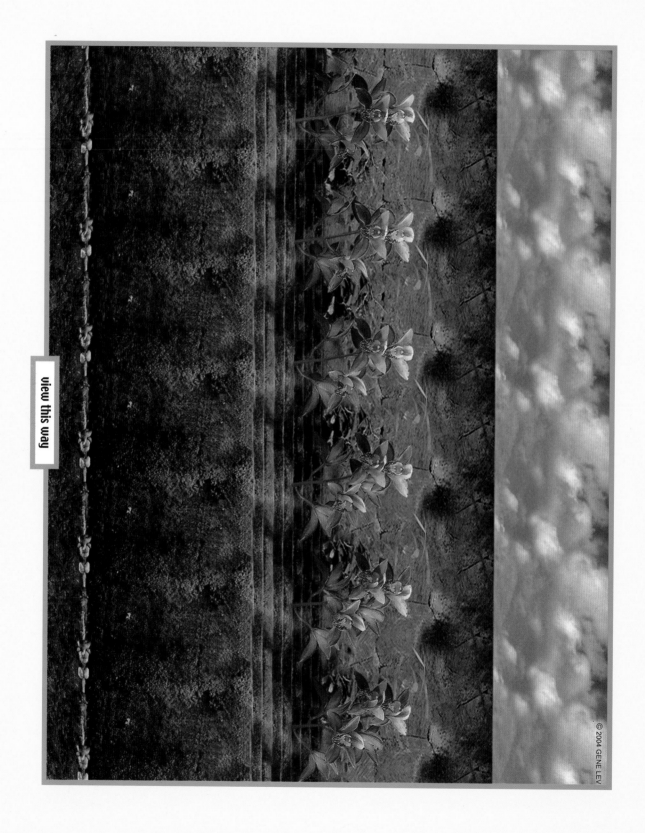

© 2004 GENE LEV

view this way

Seahorse Herd

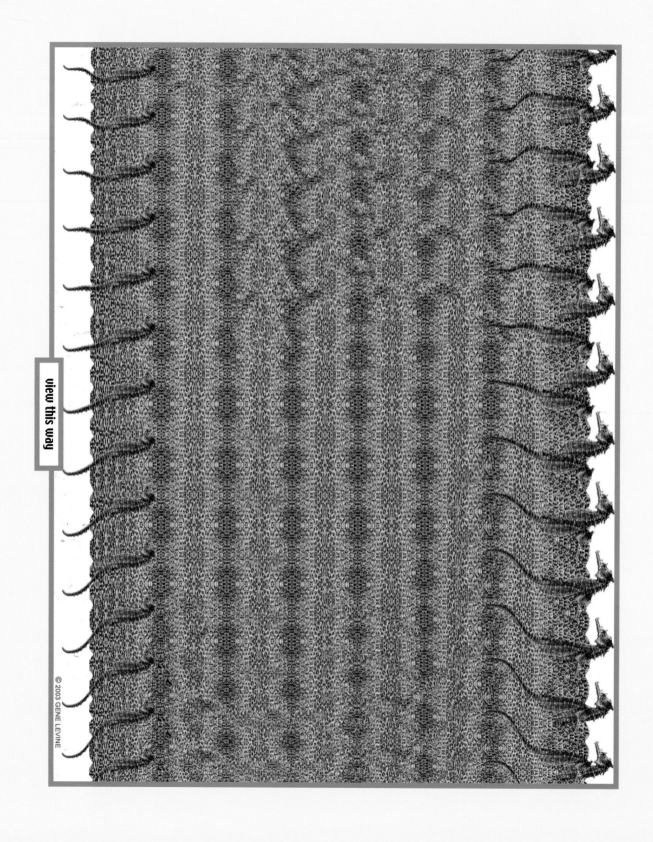

view this way

58

view this way

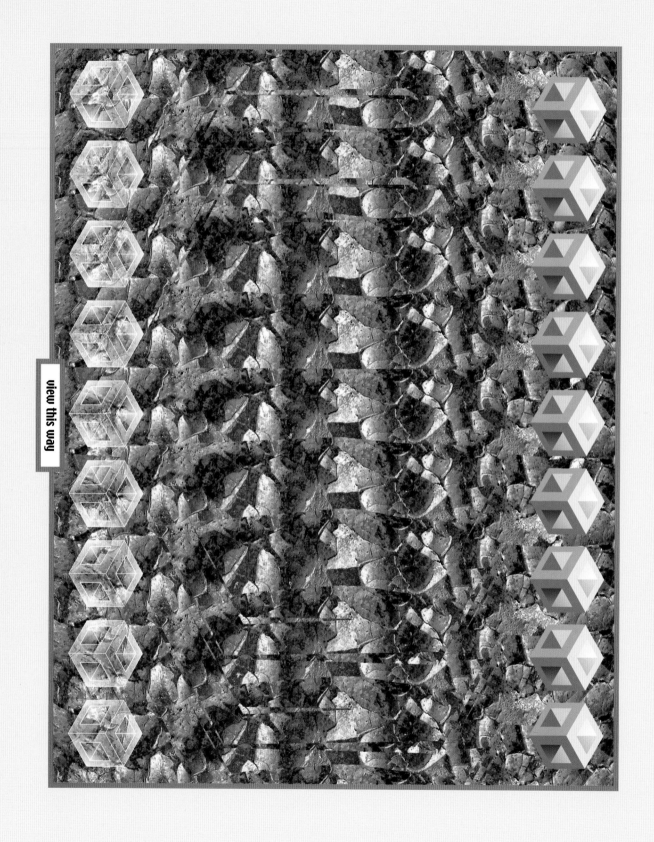

view this way

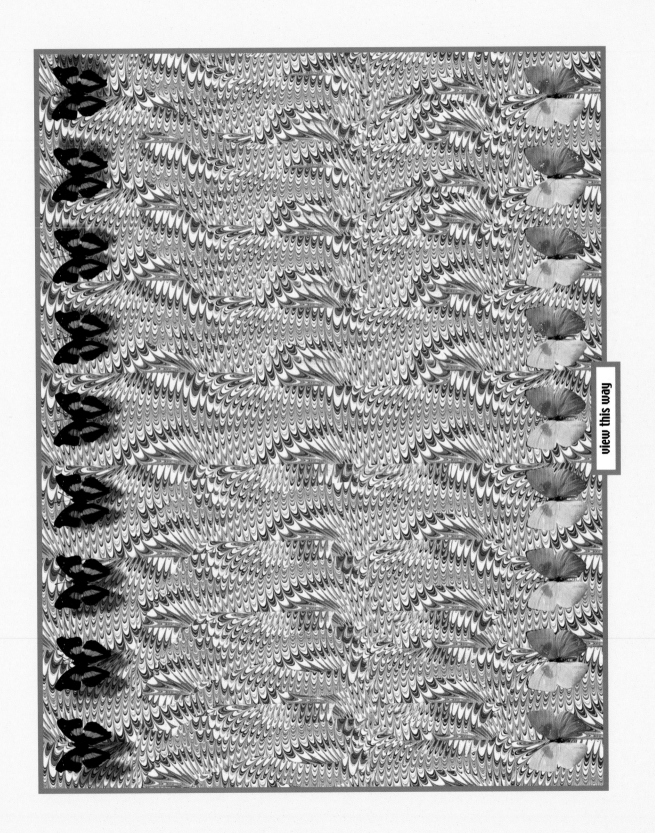

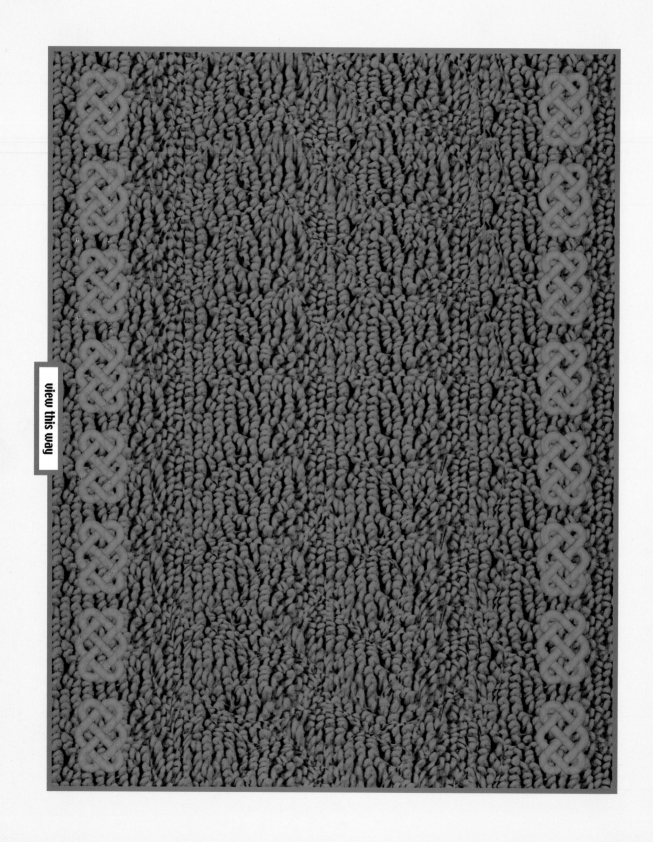

view this way

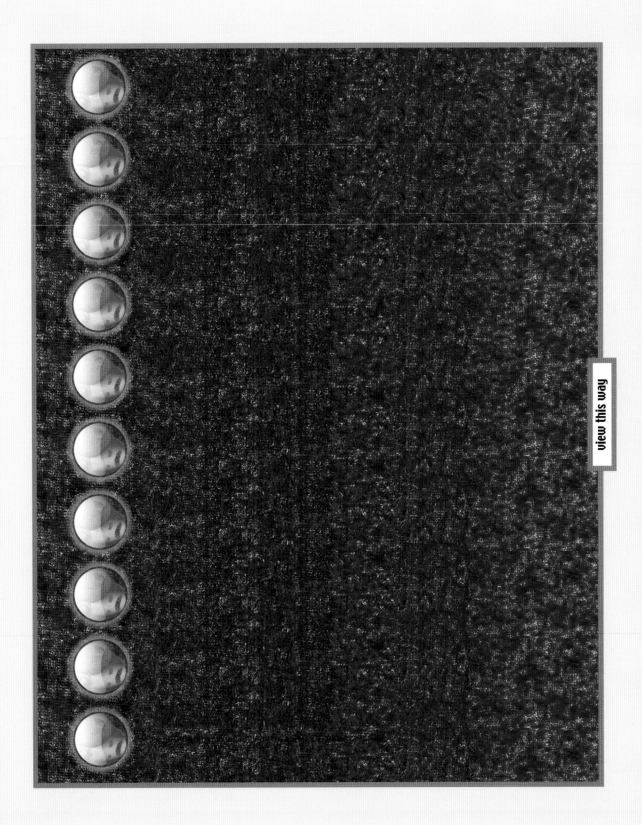

view this way

Dice

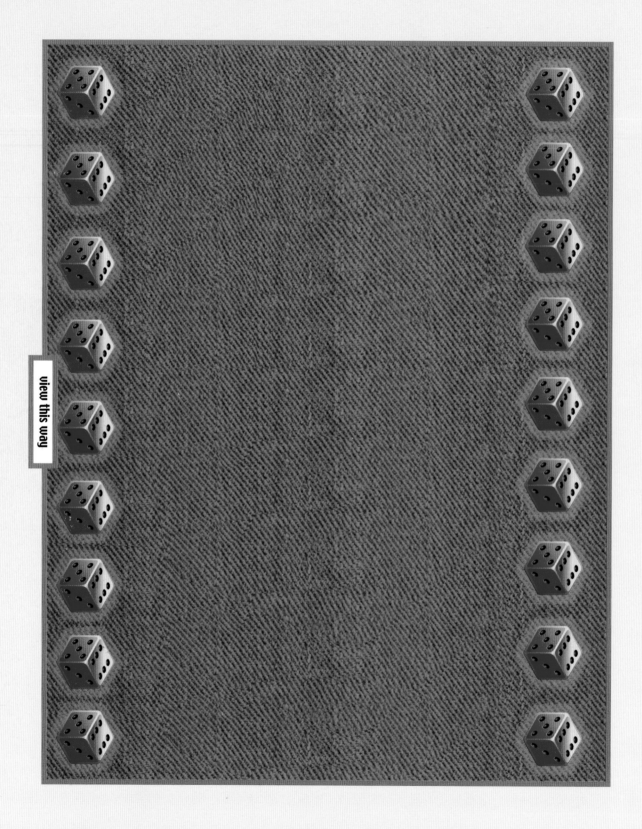

view this way

Dos Espirales

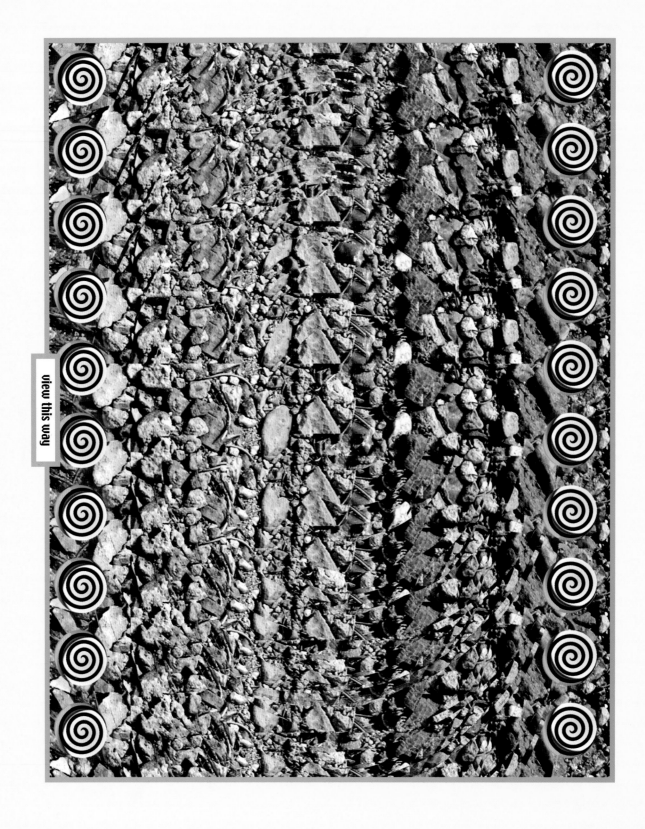

view this way

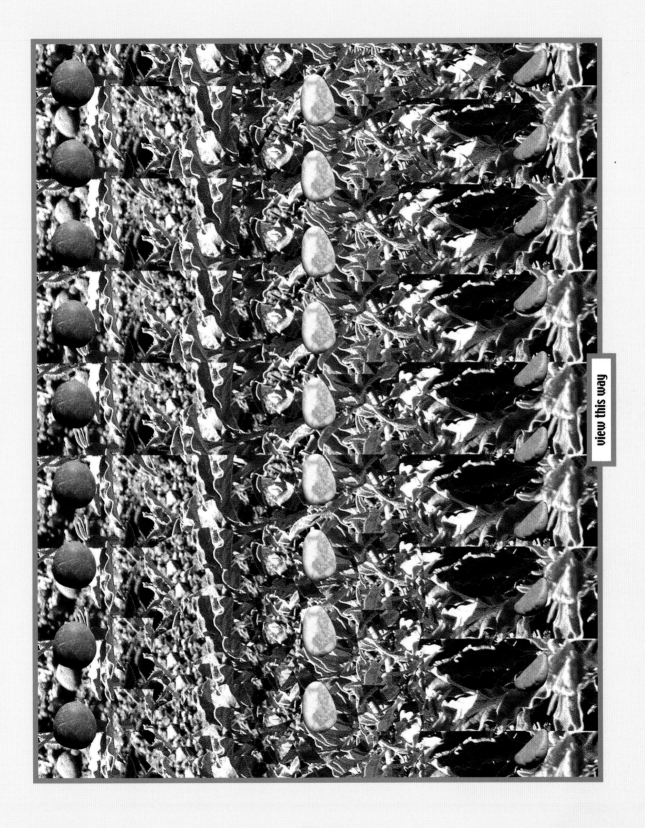

view this way

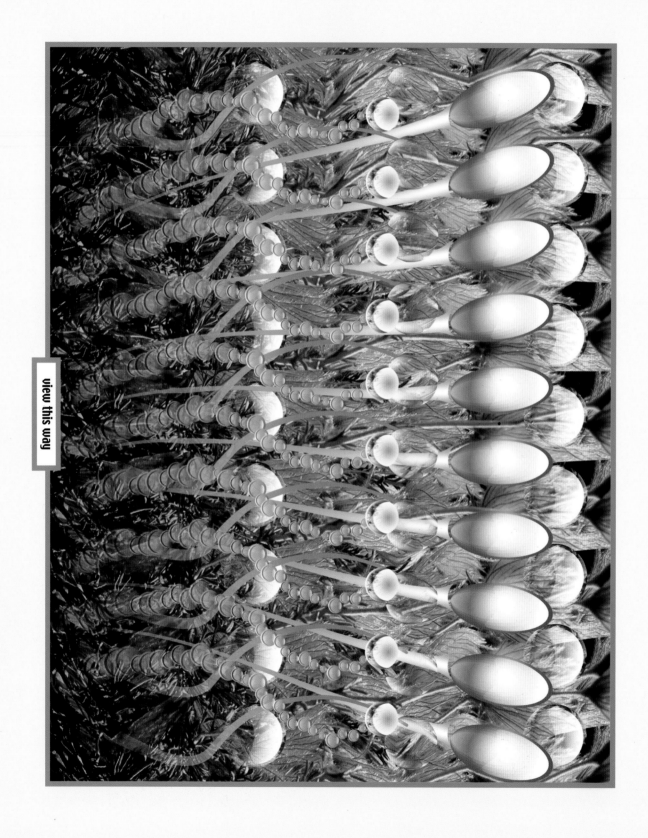

view this way

view this way

view this way

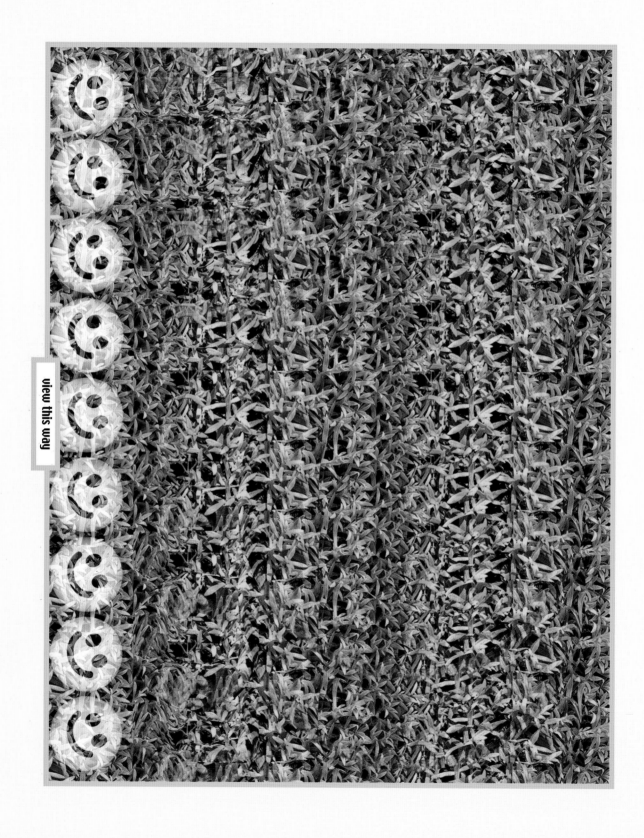

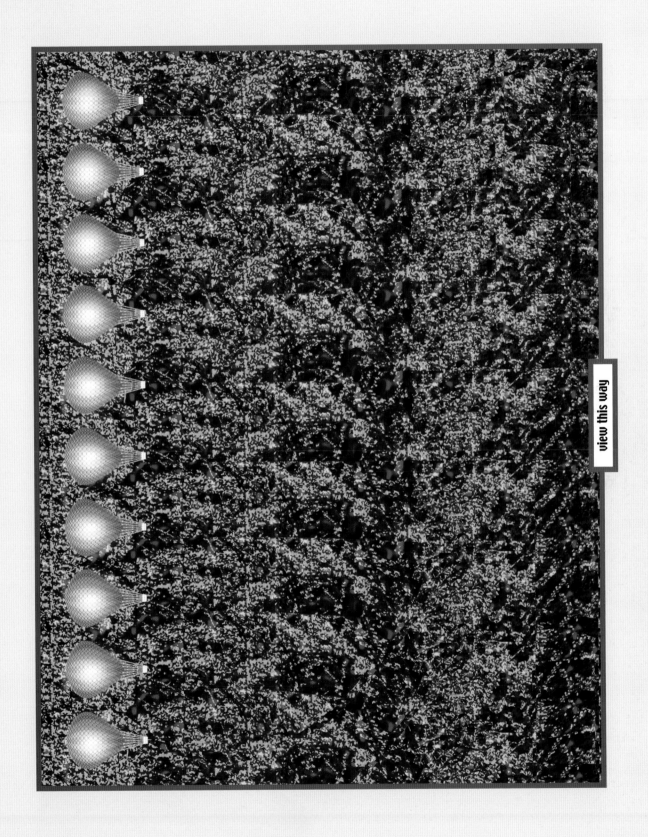

view this way

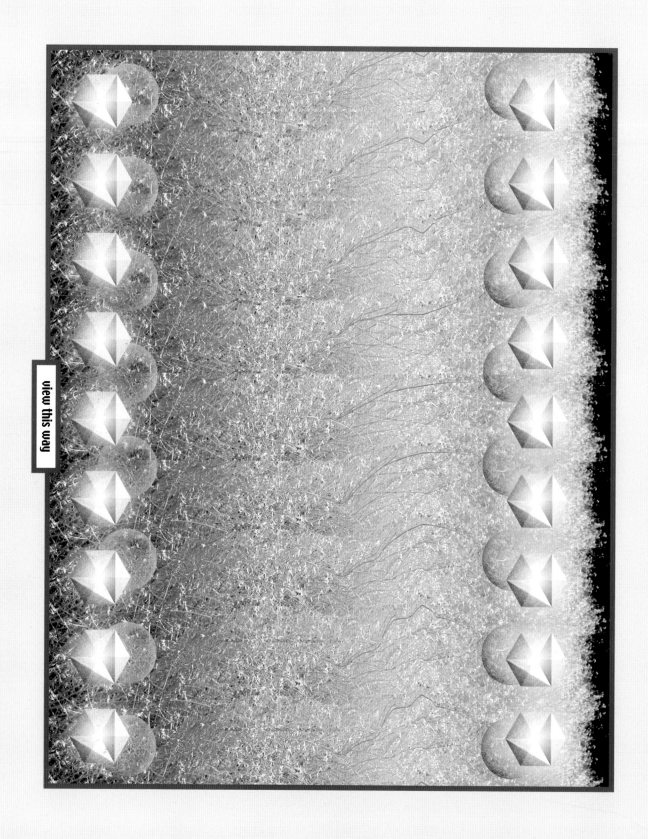

view this way

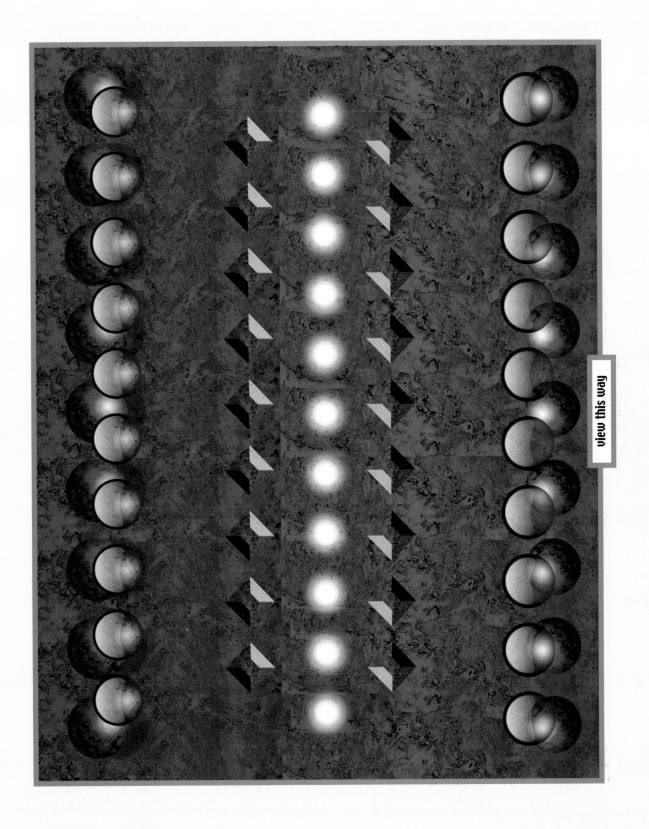

view this way

view this way

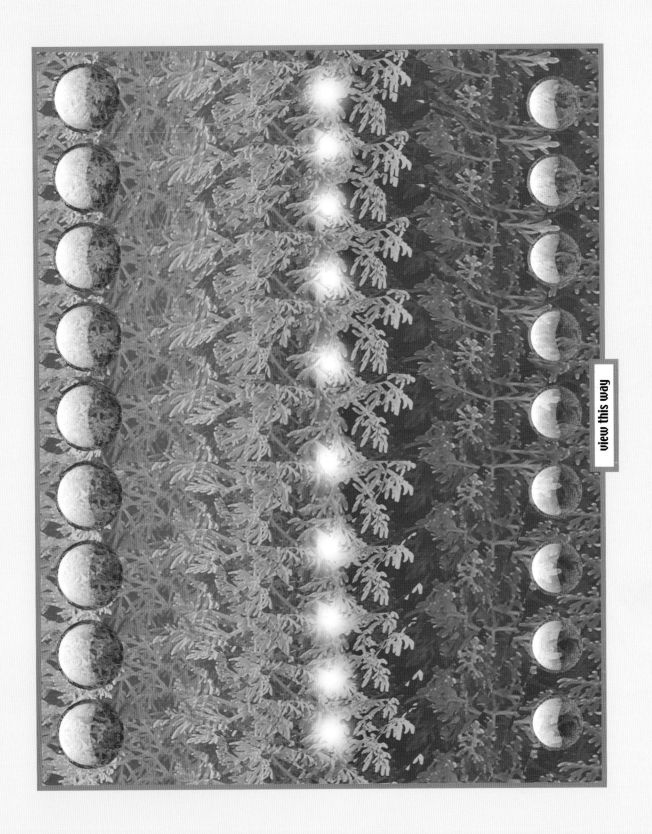

view this way

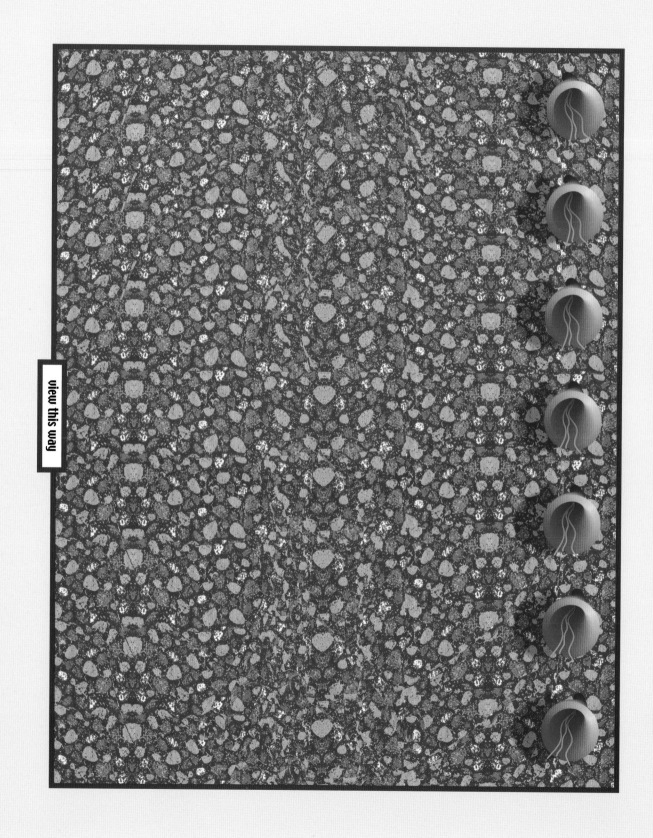

view this way

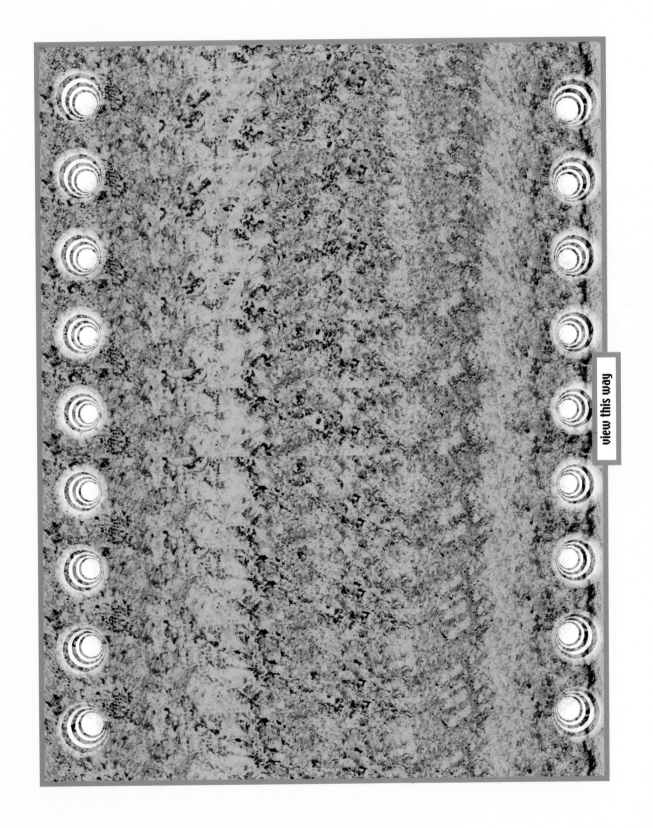

view this way

Entanglements

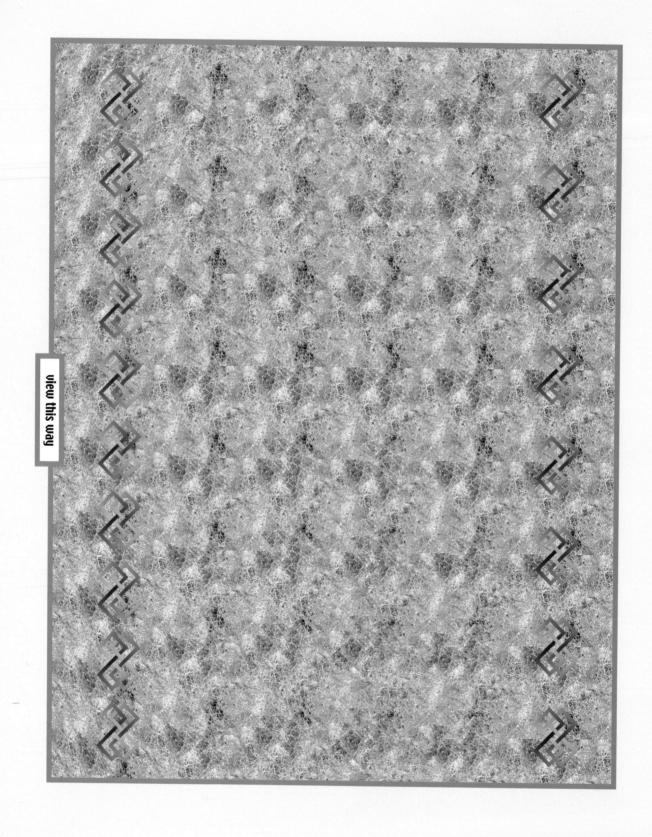

view this way

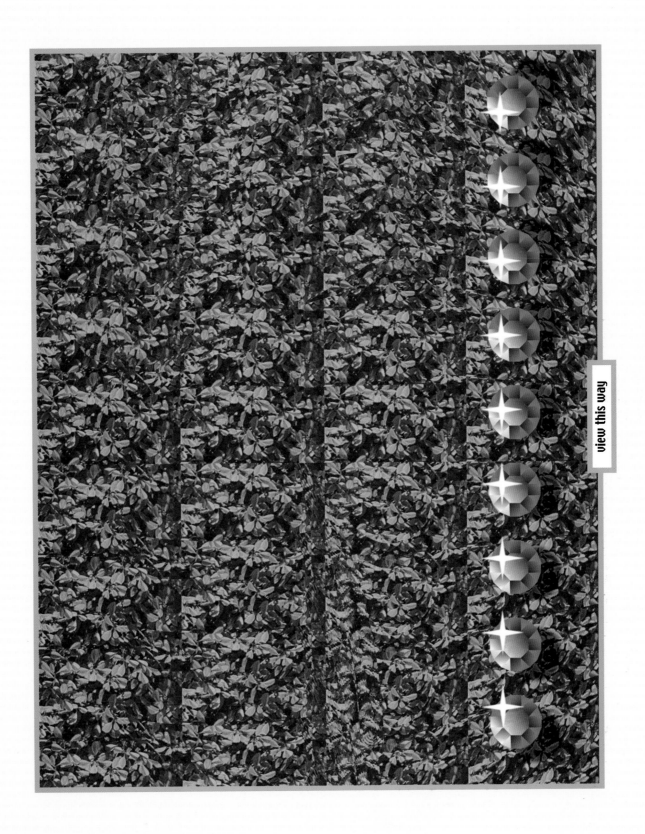

view this way

Star

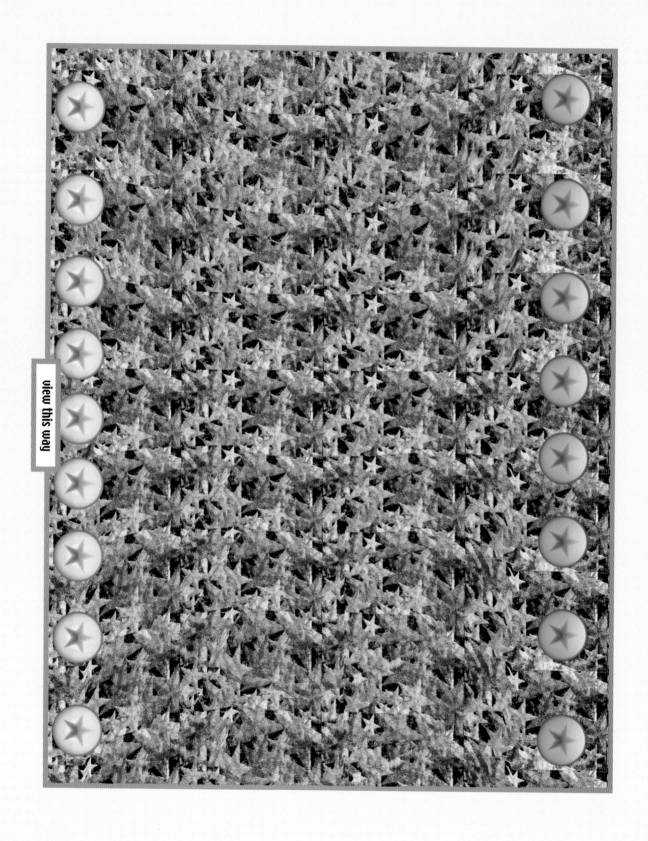

view this way

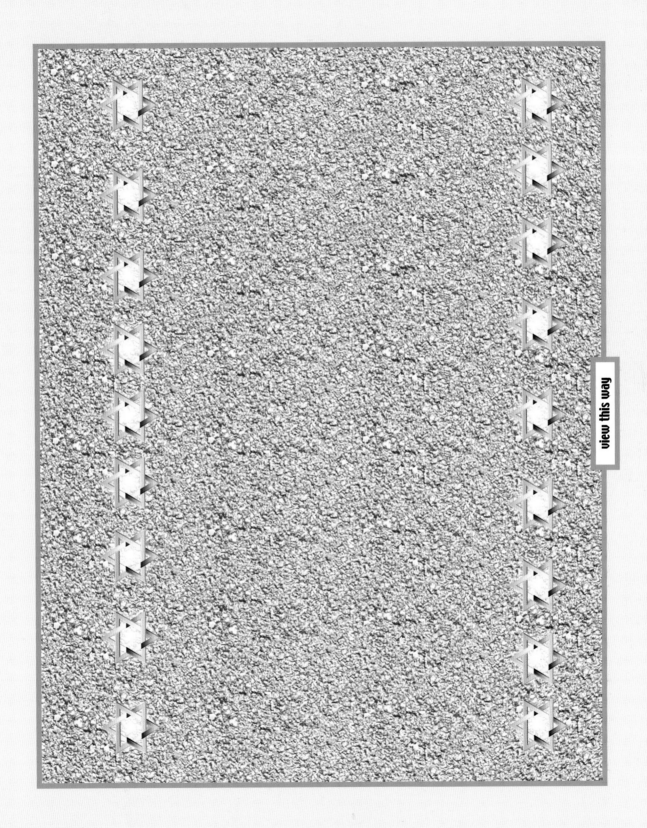

view this way

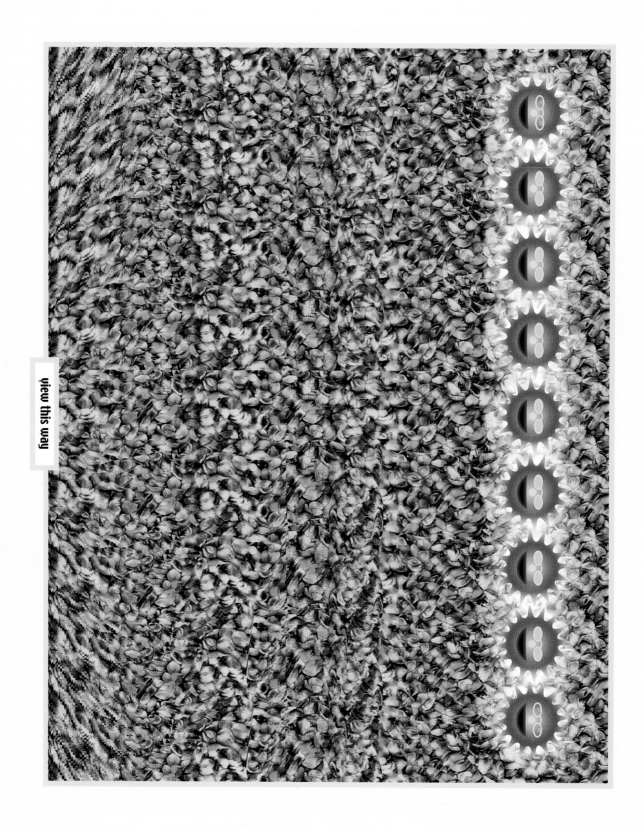

view this way

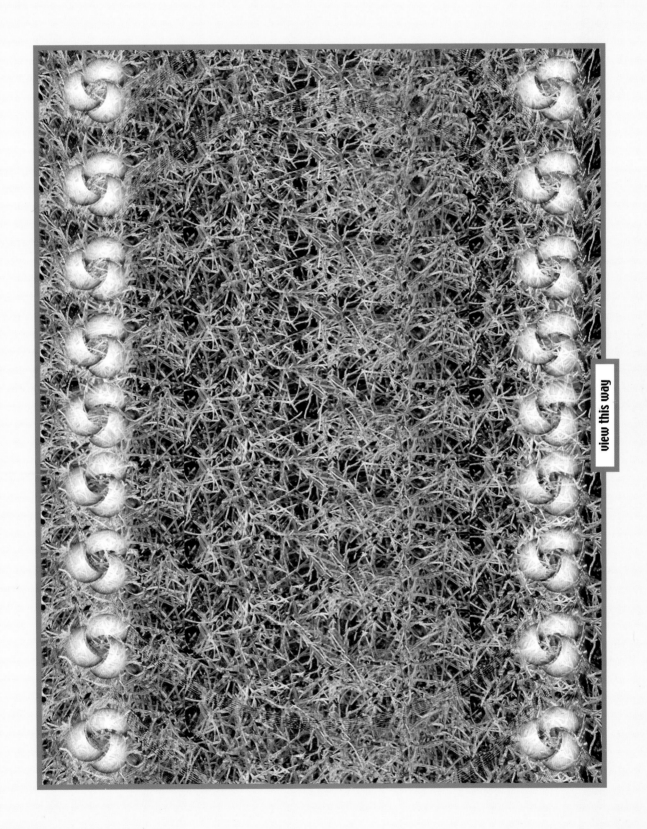

view this way

Trilogy 2

view this way

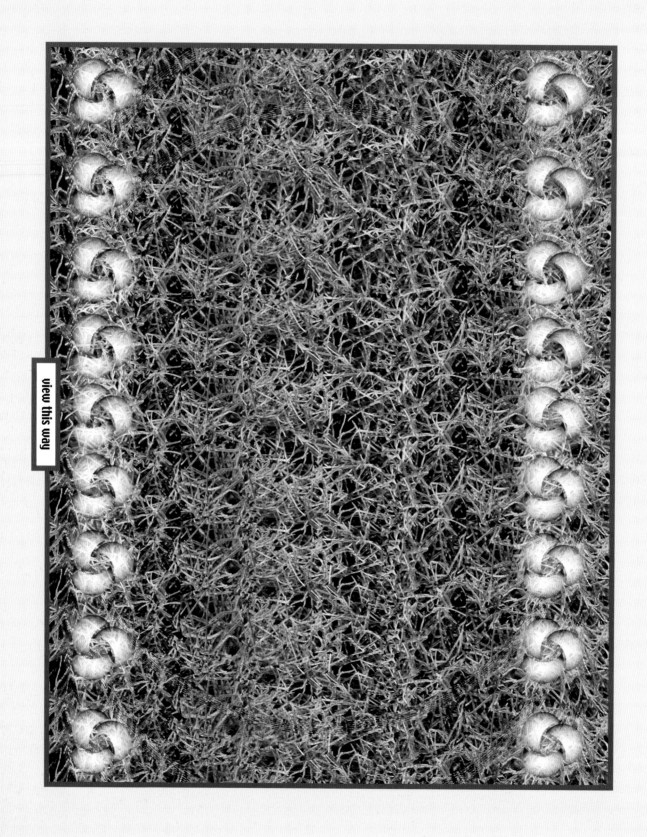

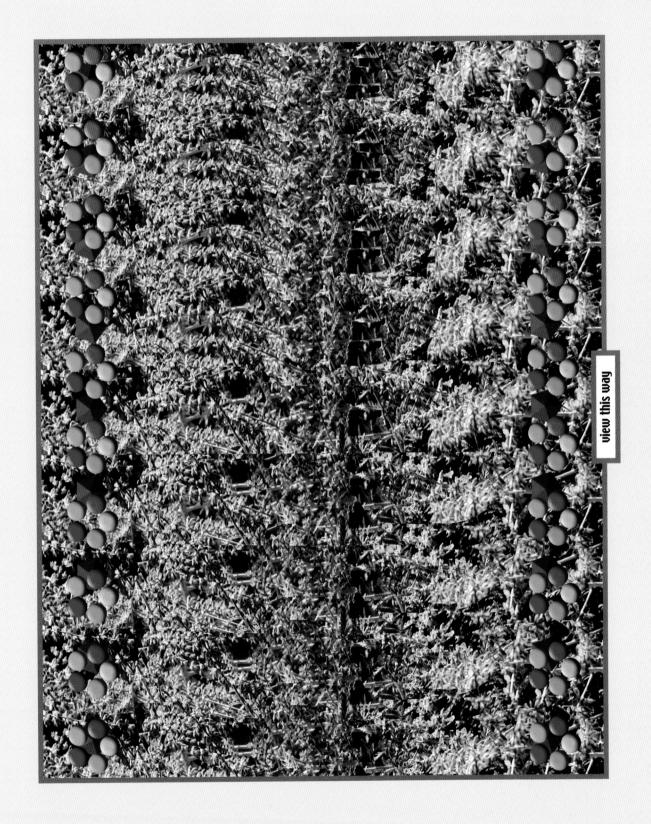

view this way

Anasazi Petroglyphs

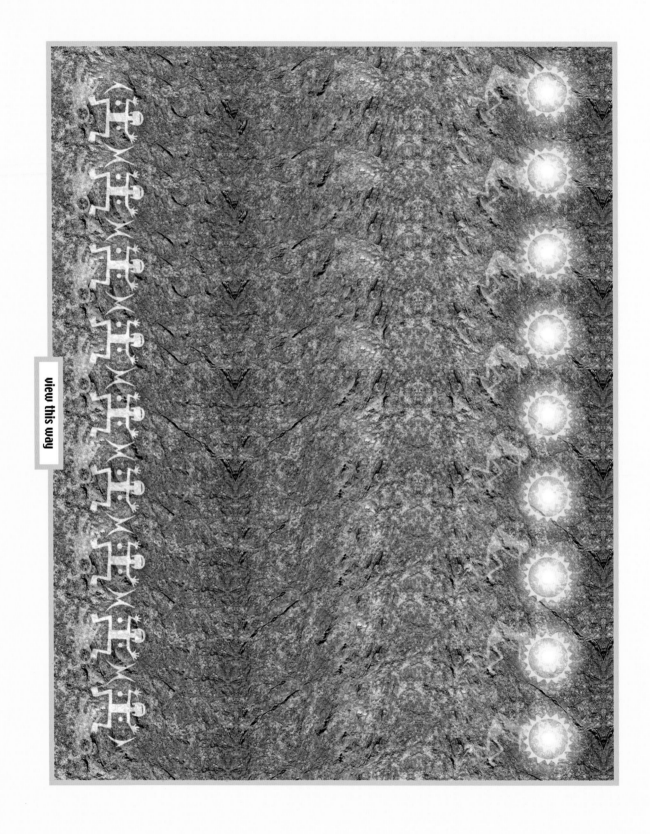

view this way

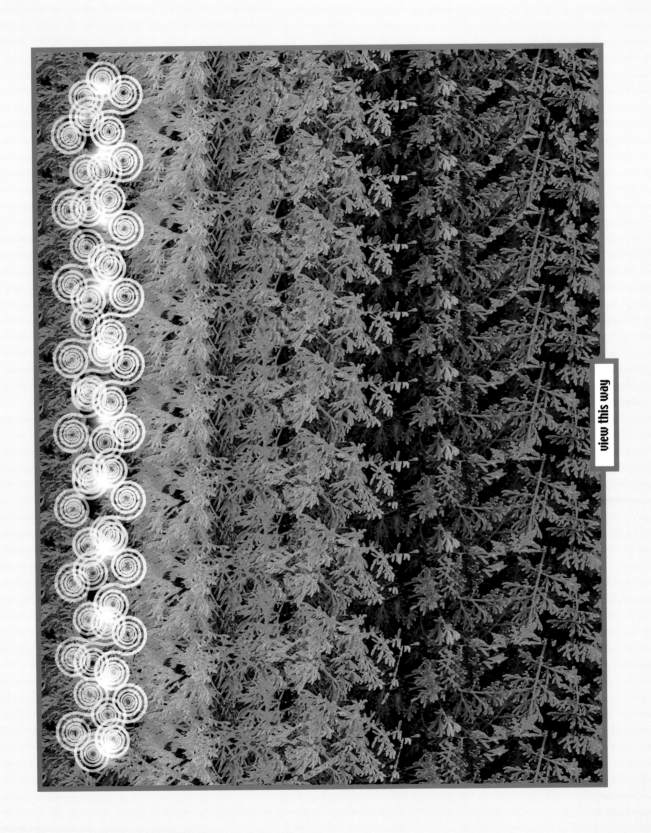

view this way

Cards

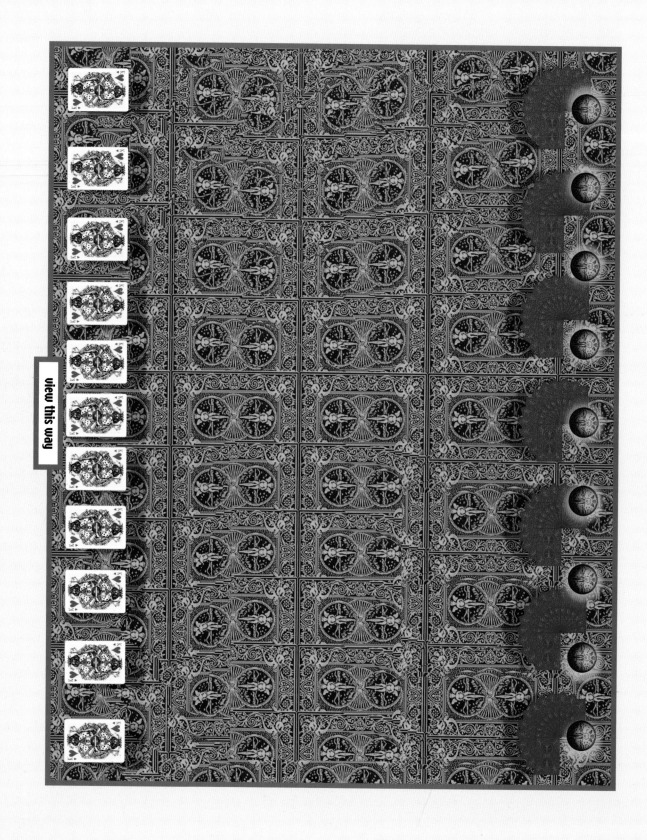

view this way

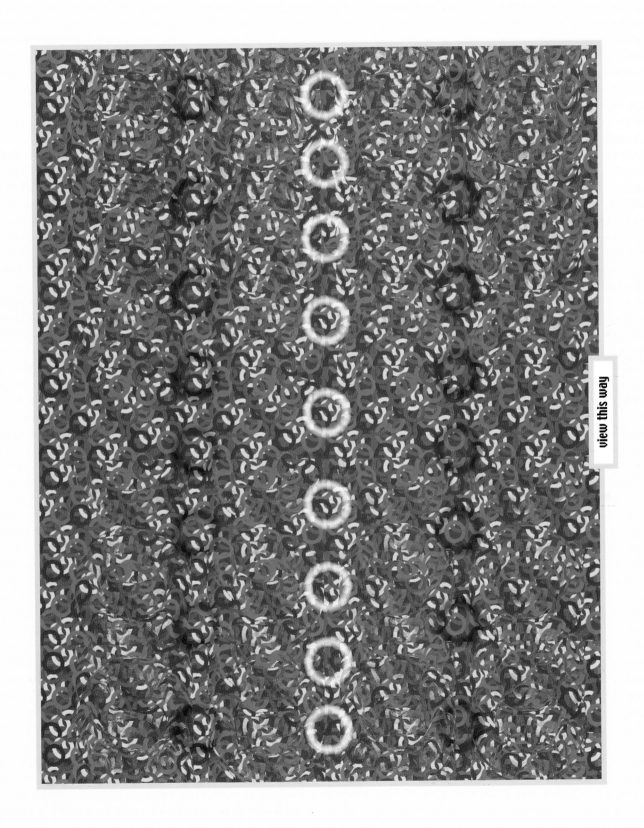

view this way

Cube & Hoop

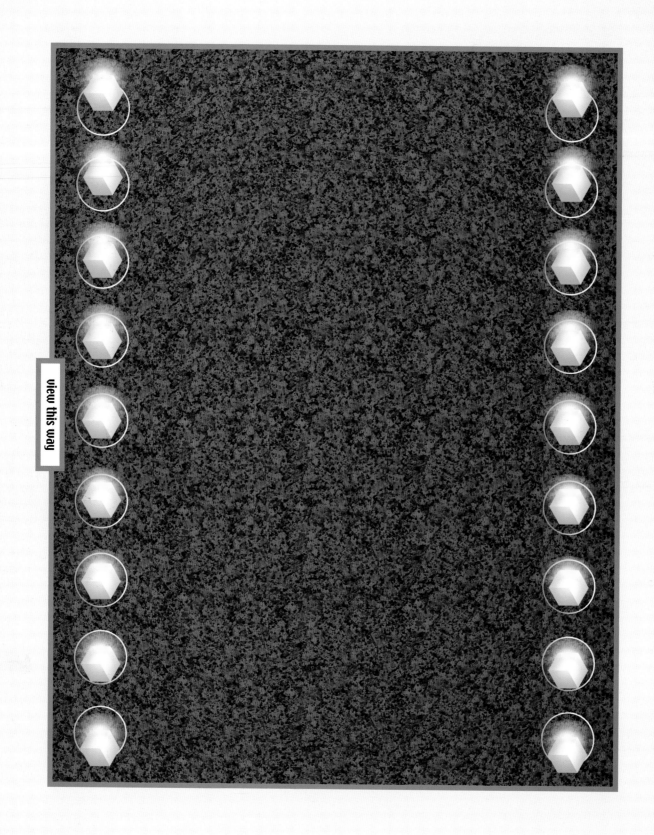

view this way

90

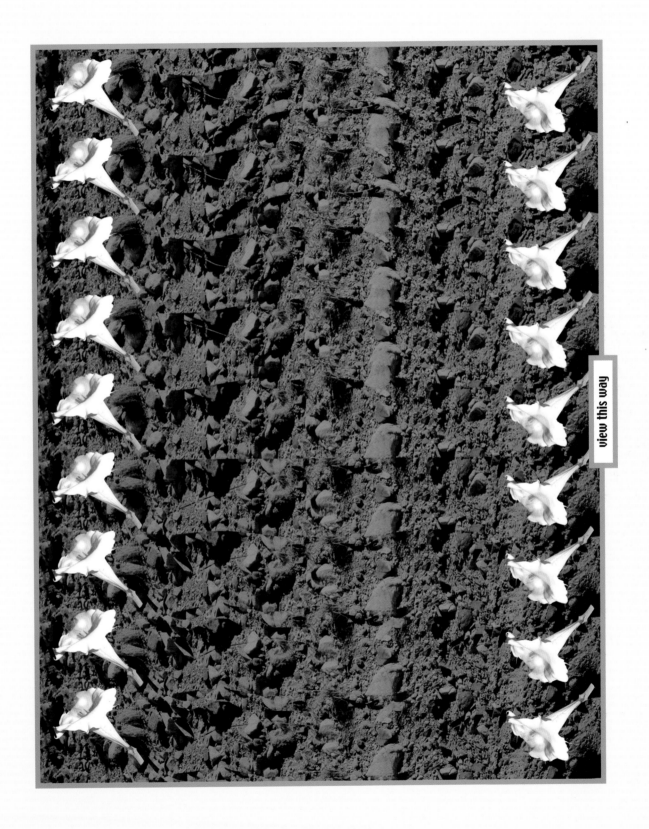

view this way

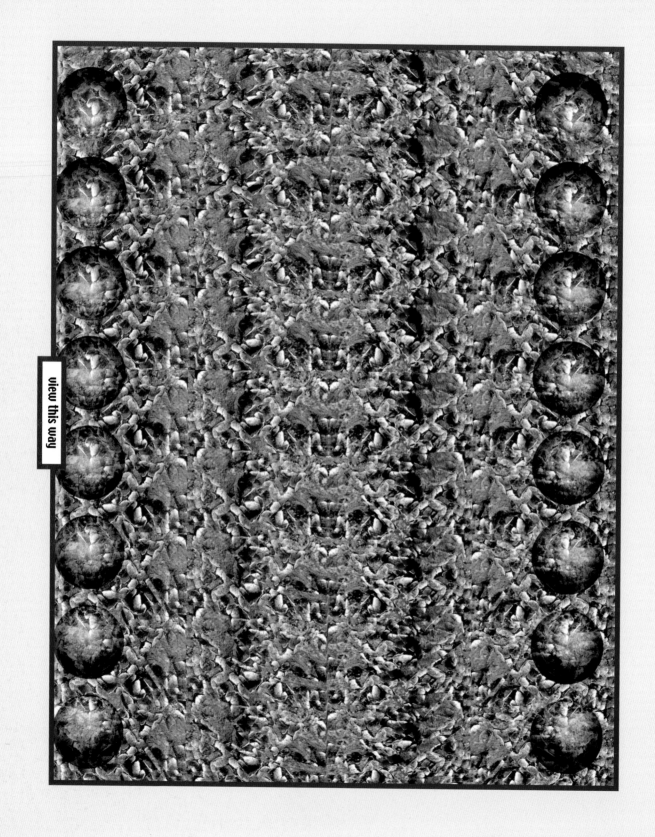

view this way

view this way

Golden Medley

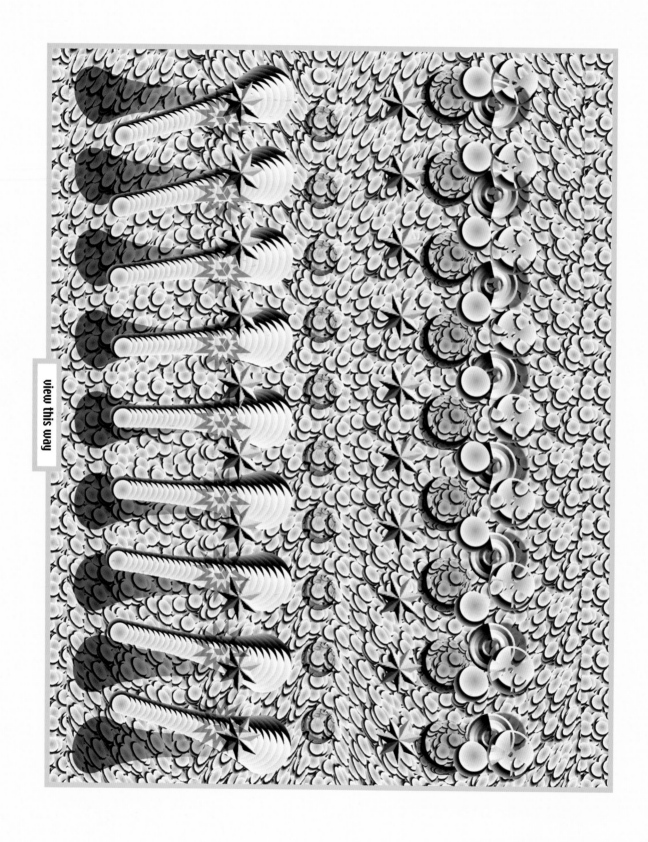

view this way

94

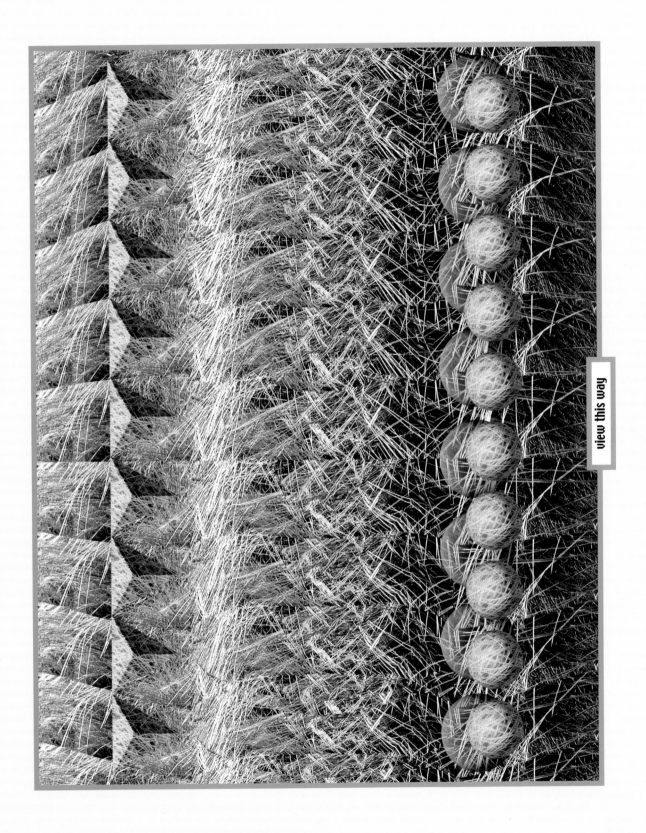

view this way

Hole in my Heart

view this way

96

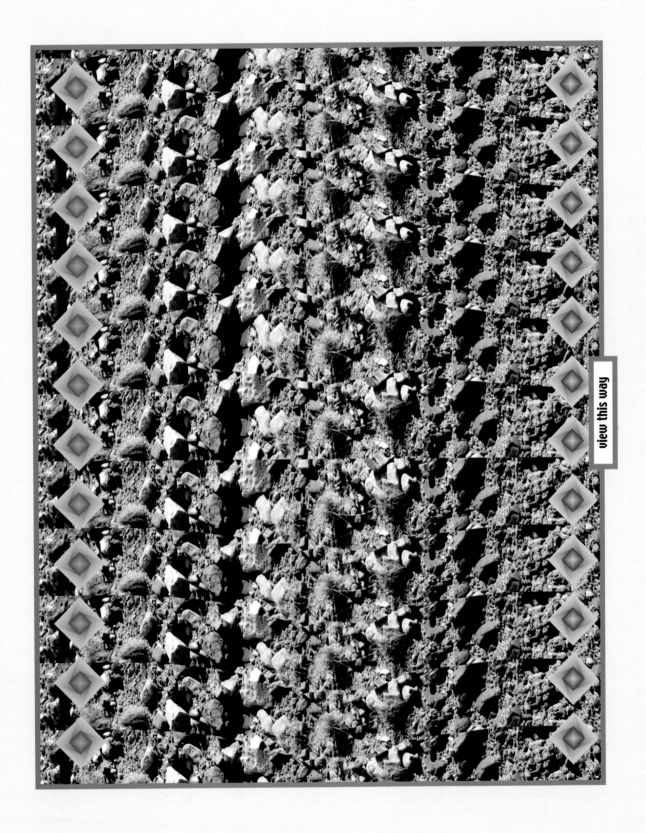

view this way

Interlocking Stars

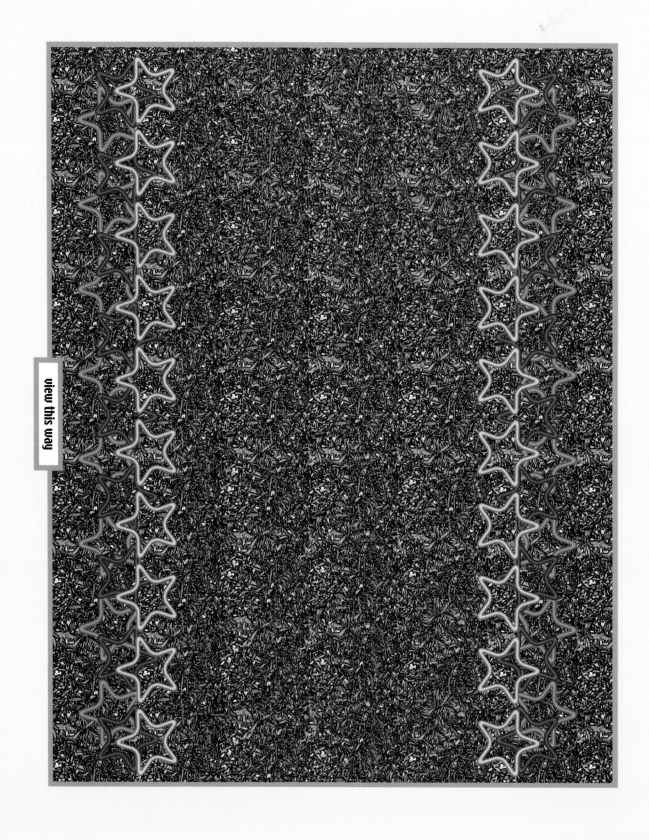

view this way

view this way

Officer Winkie

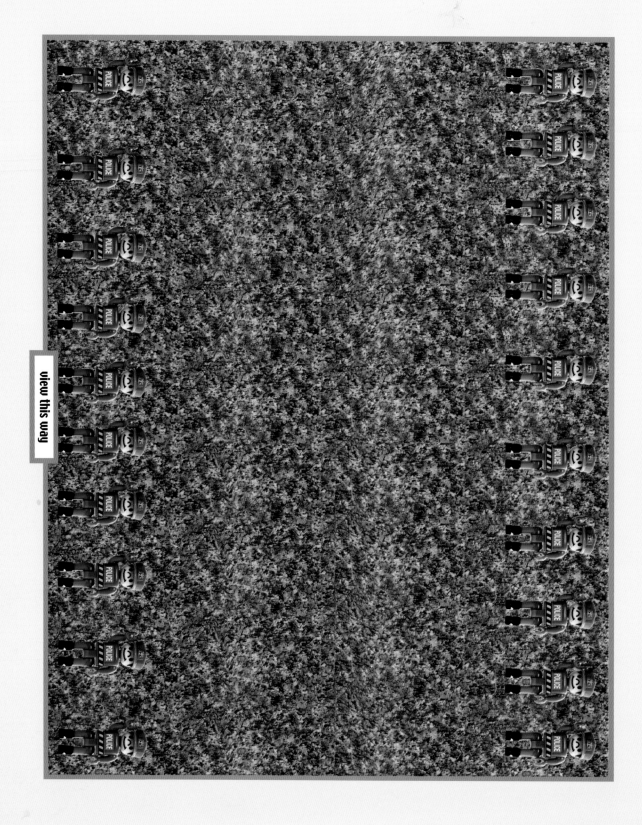

view this way

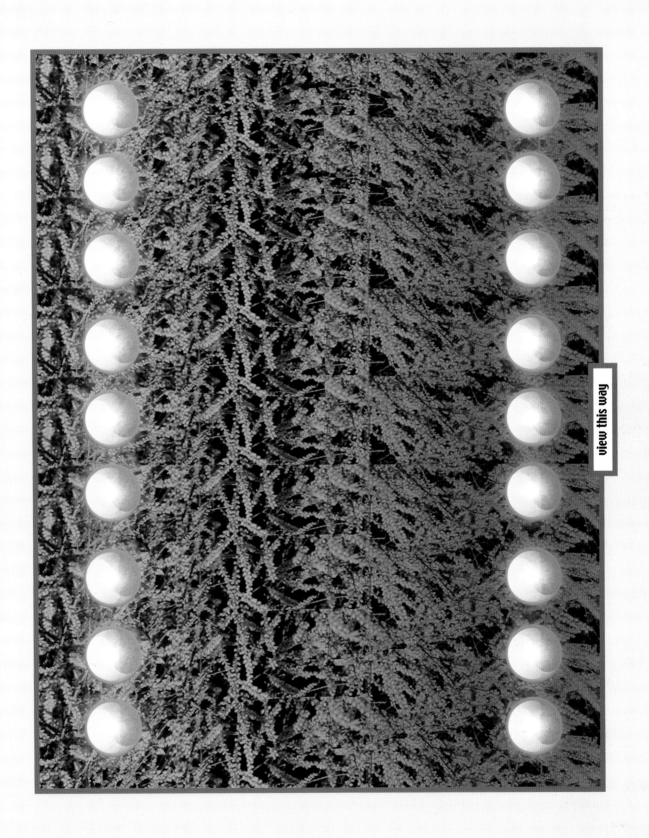

view this way

Pluses

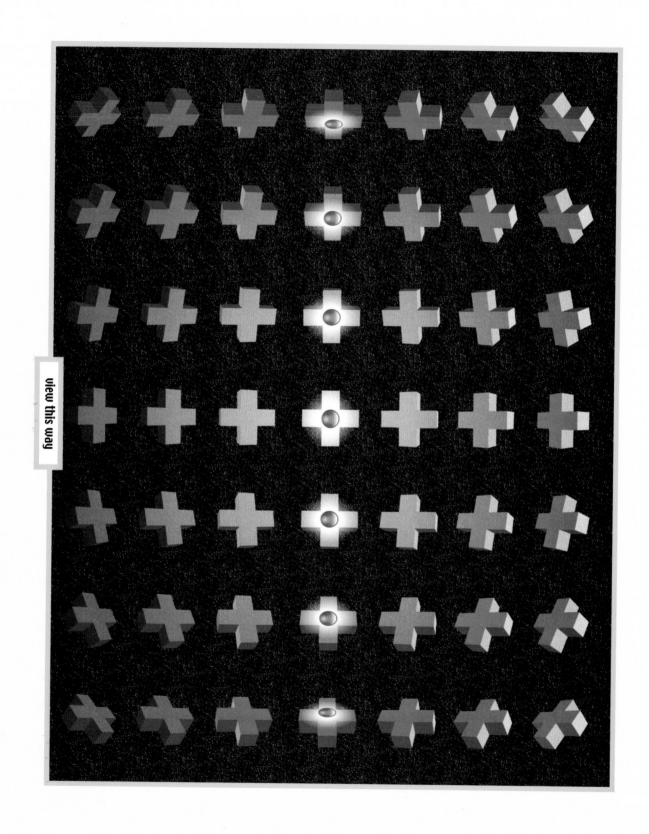

view this way

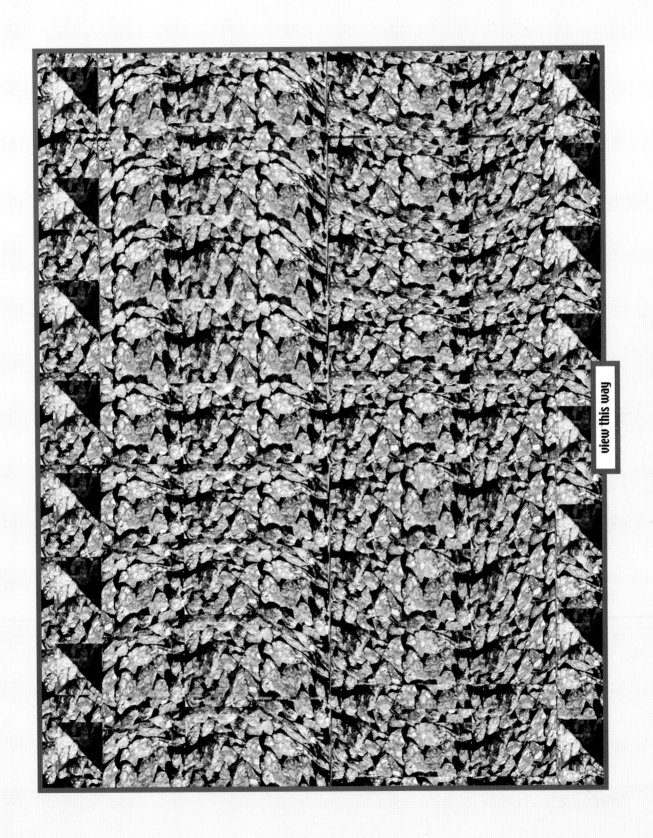

view this way

Spirals – In & Out

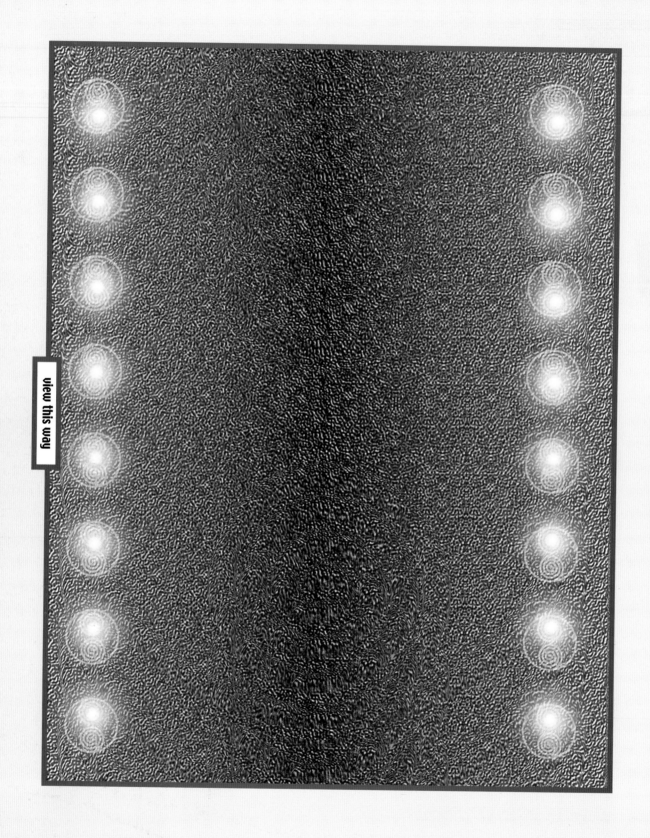

view this way

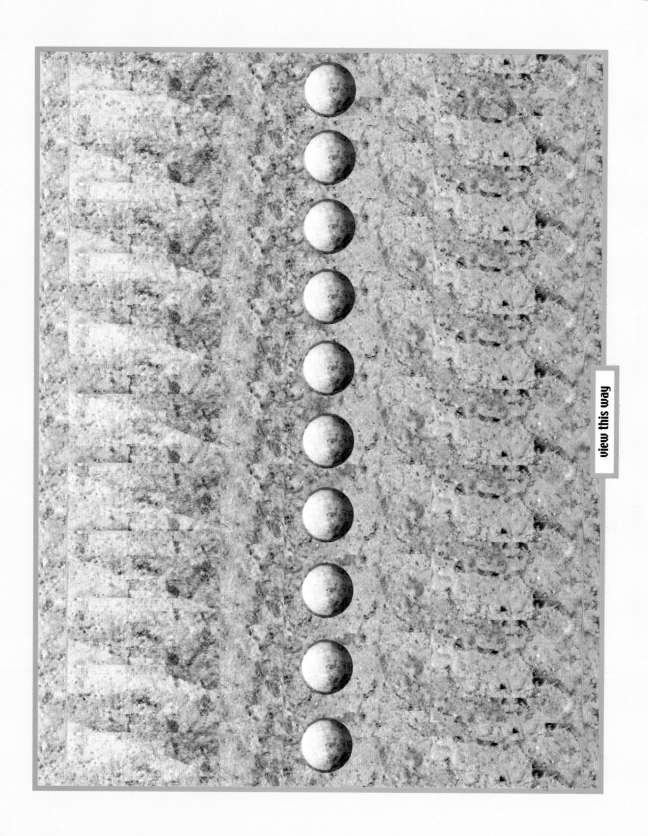

view this way

Infinity 1

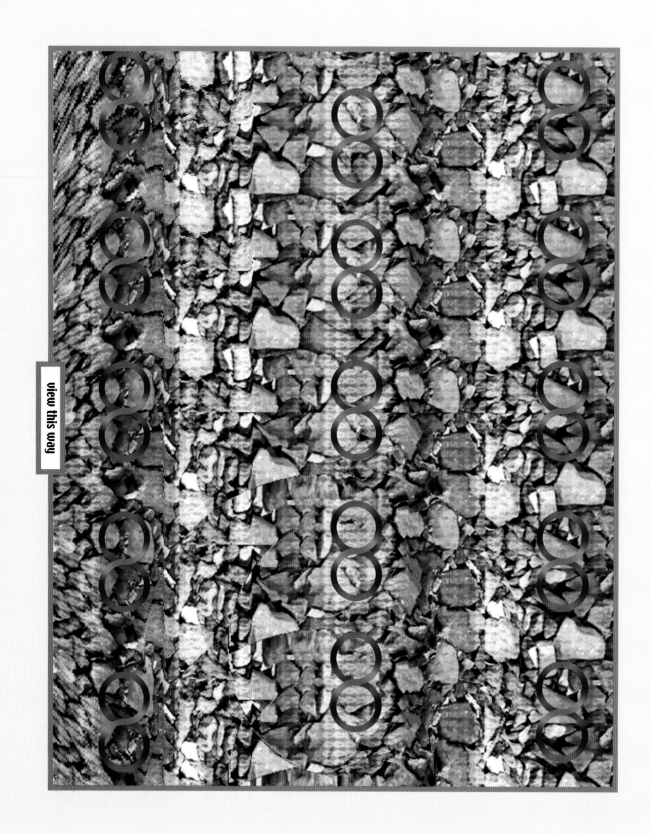

view this way

106

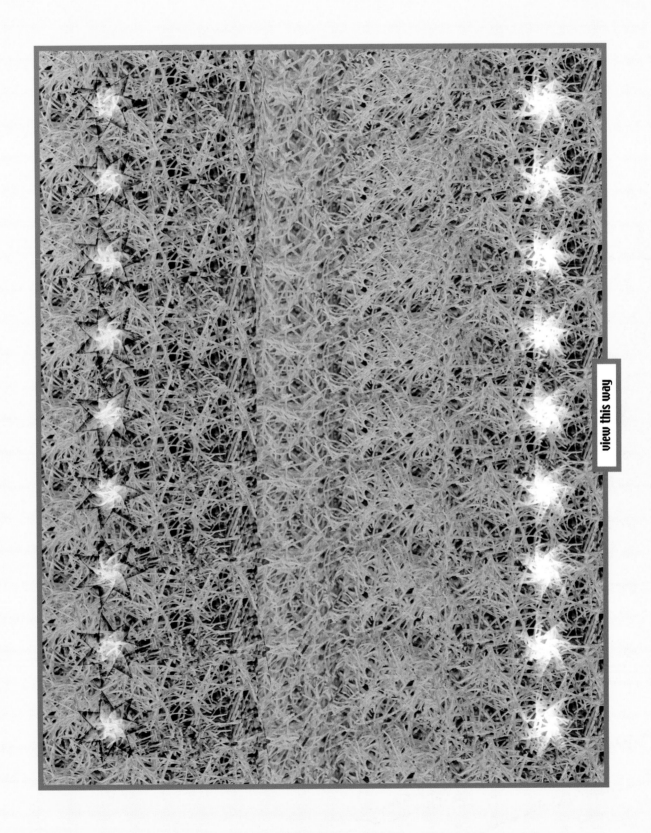

view this way

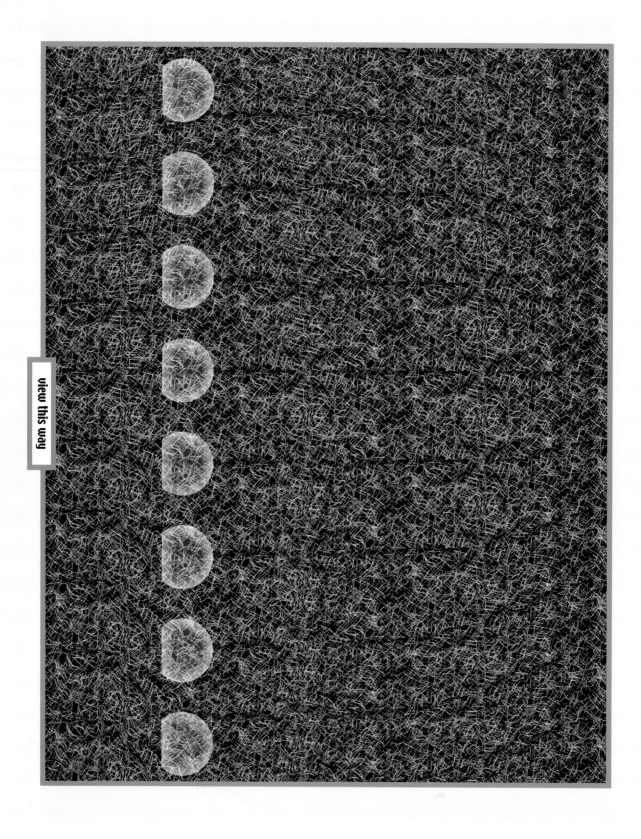

view this way

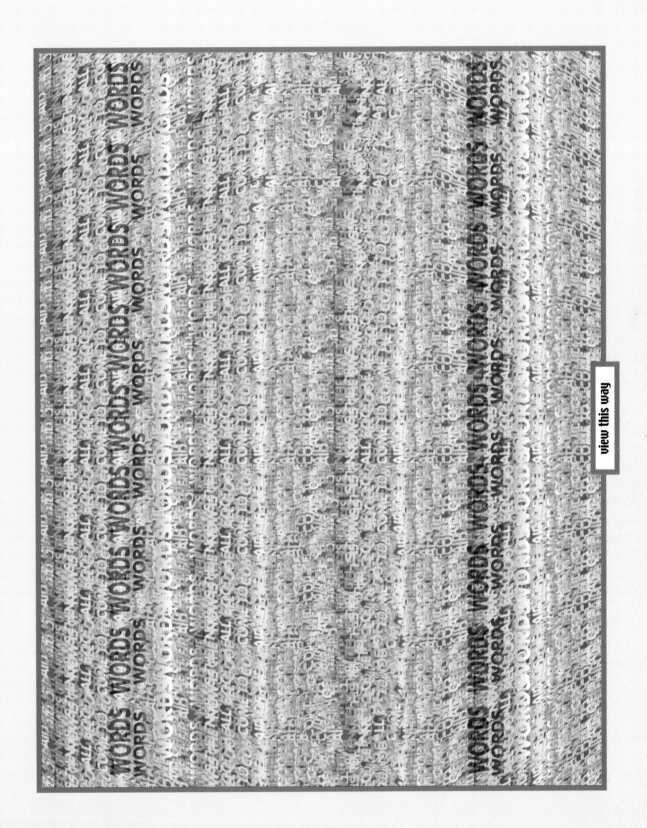

view this way

Winter Trees

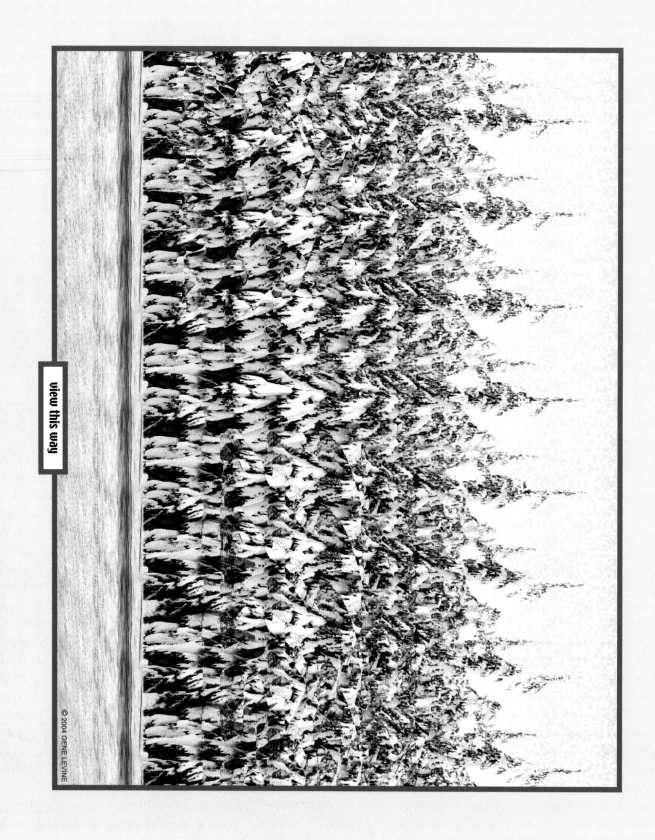

view this way

© 2004 GENE LEVINE

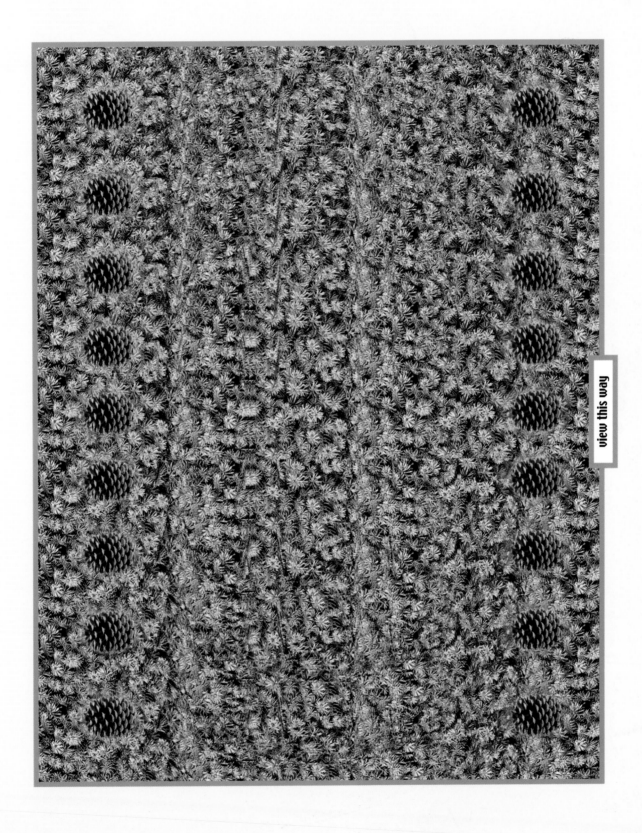

view this way

Magic Cube

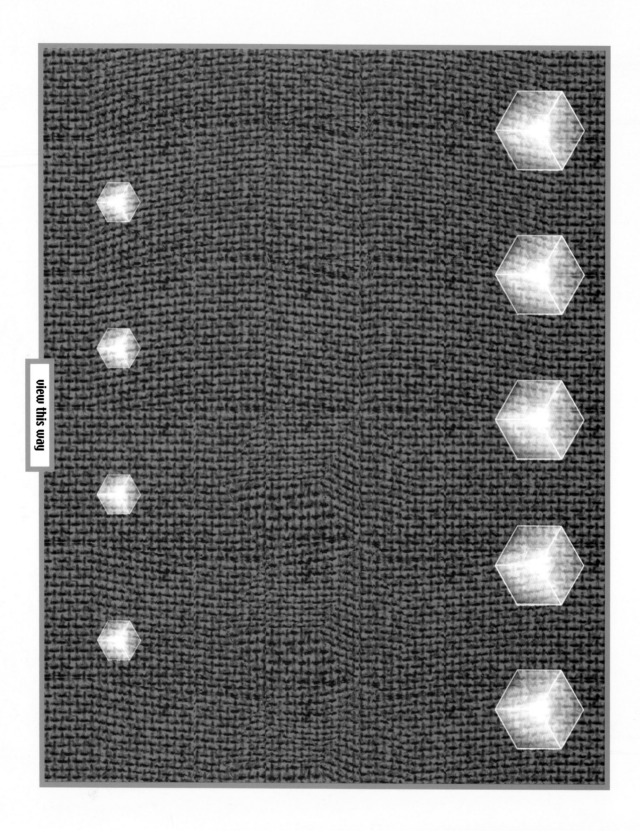

view this way

view this way

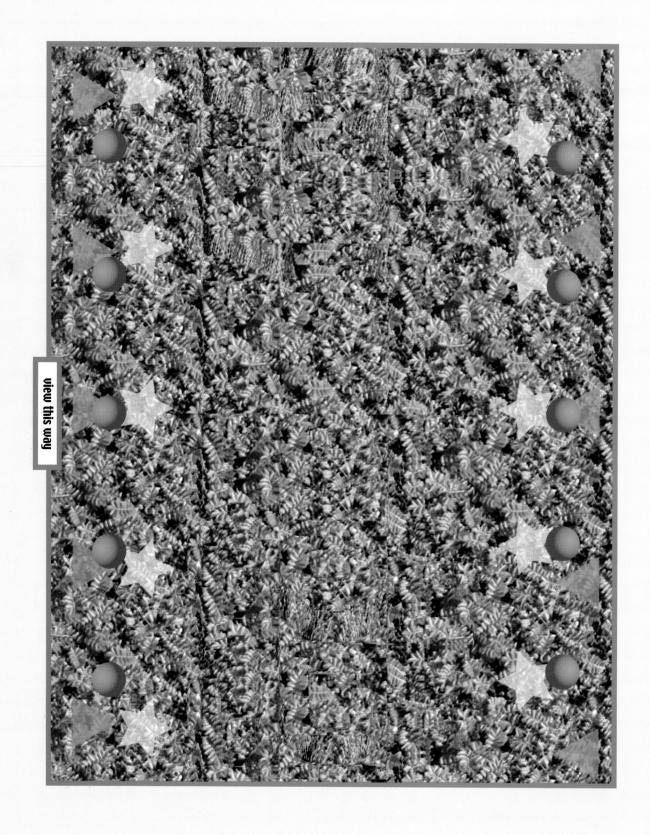

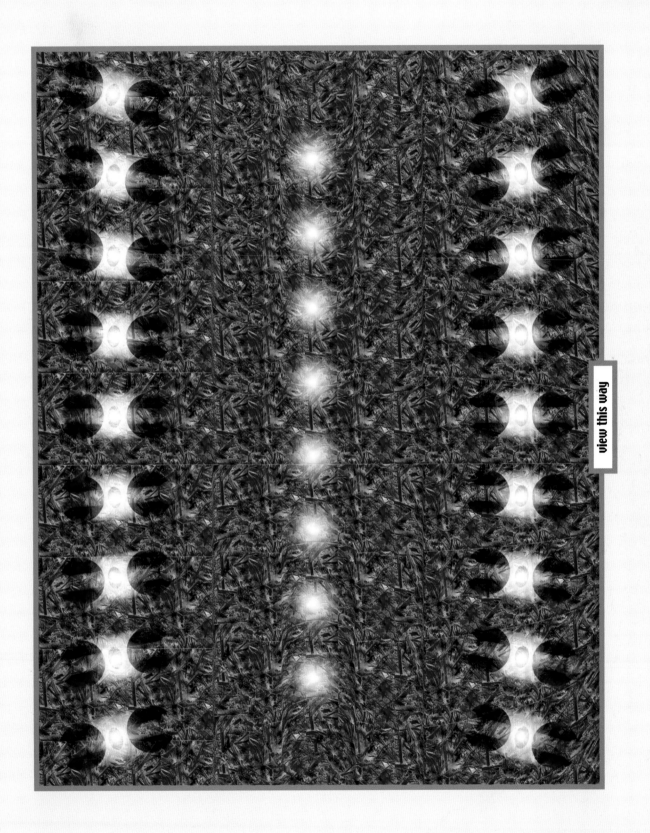

view this way

Owl

view this way

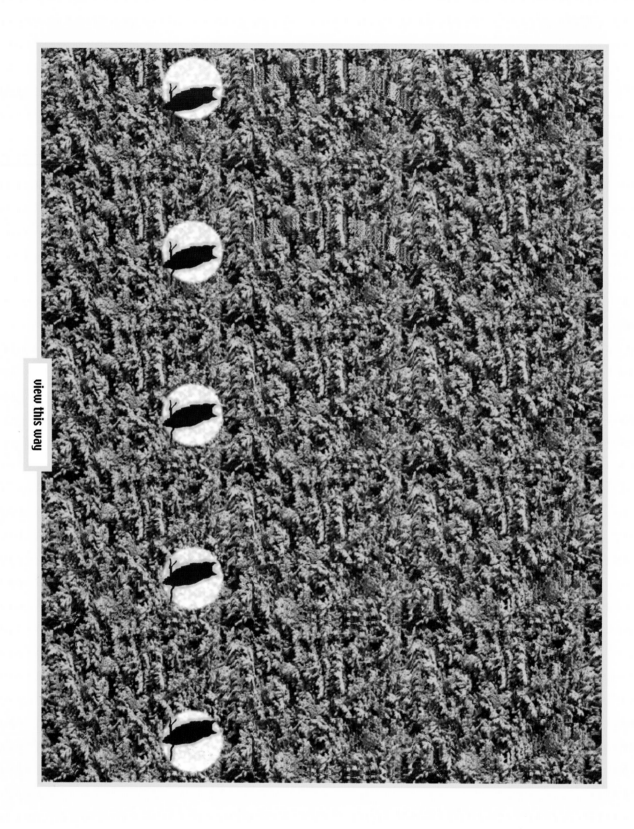

116

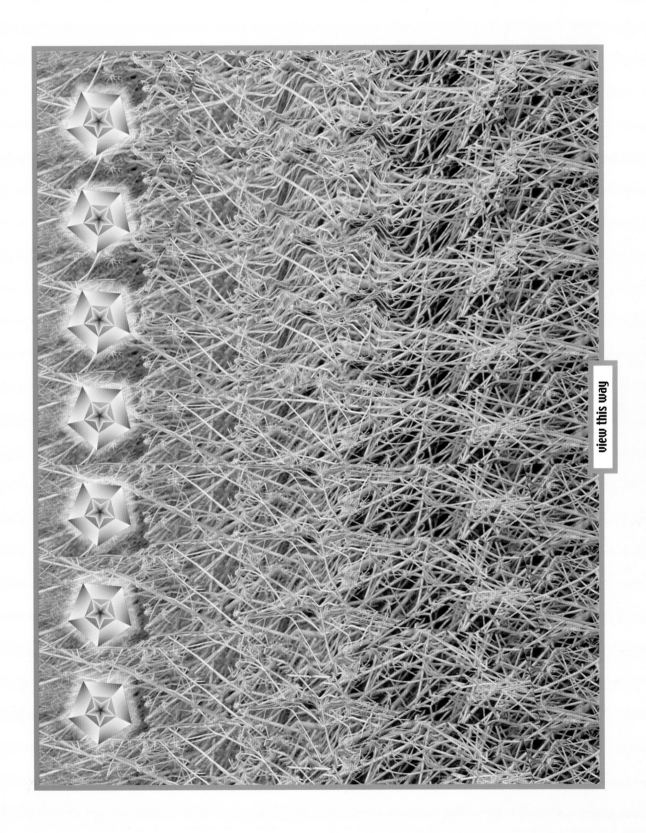

view this way

Pine Wedges

view this way

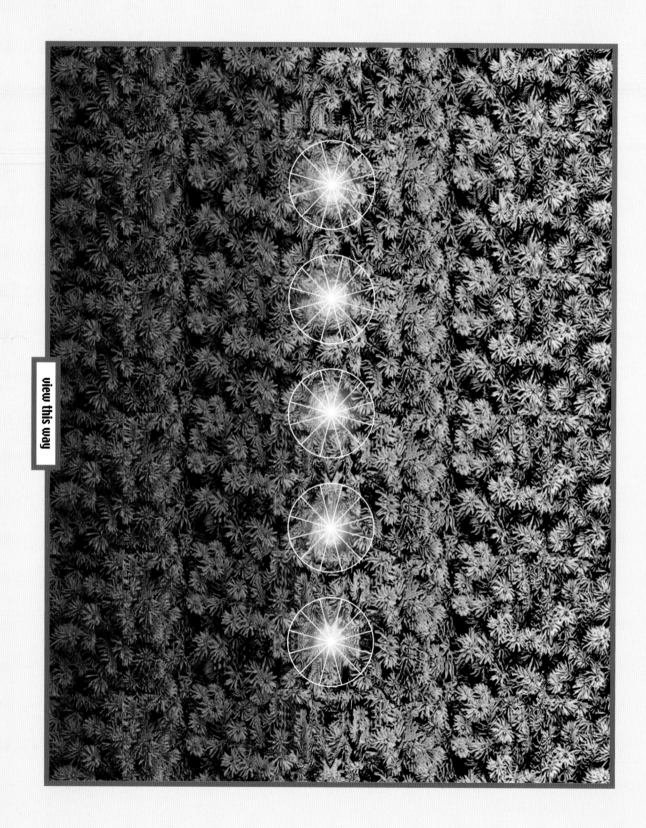

view this way

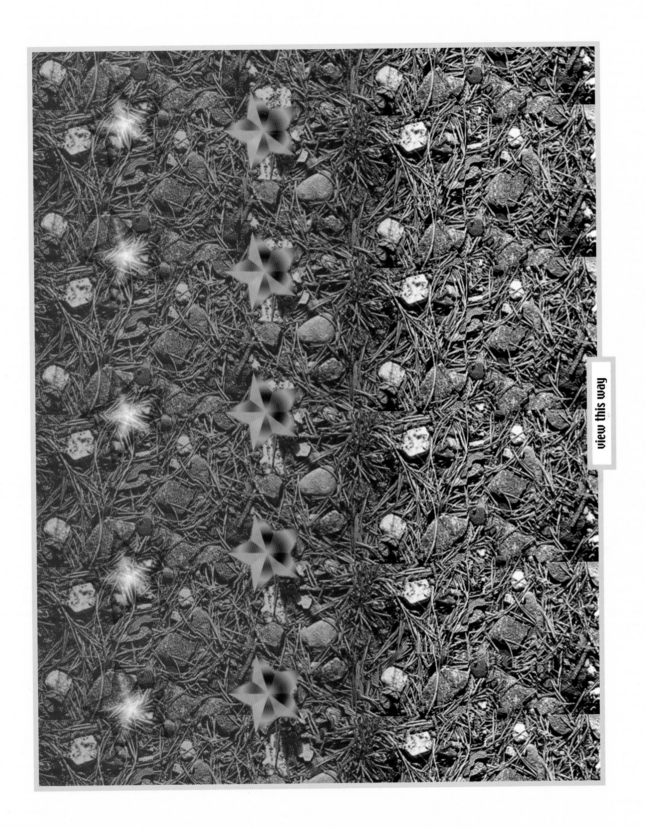

view this way

Snow Angel

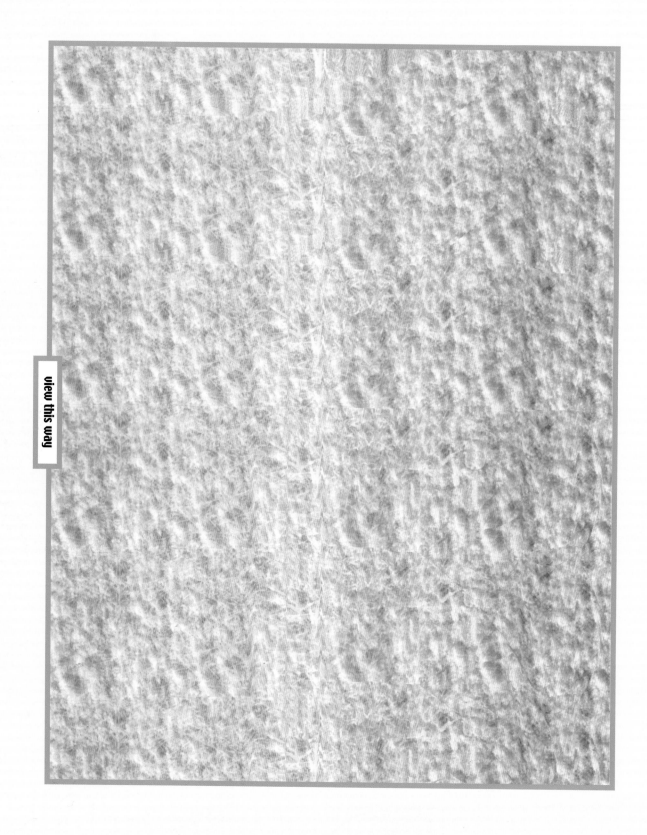

view this way

view this way

Rock Star

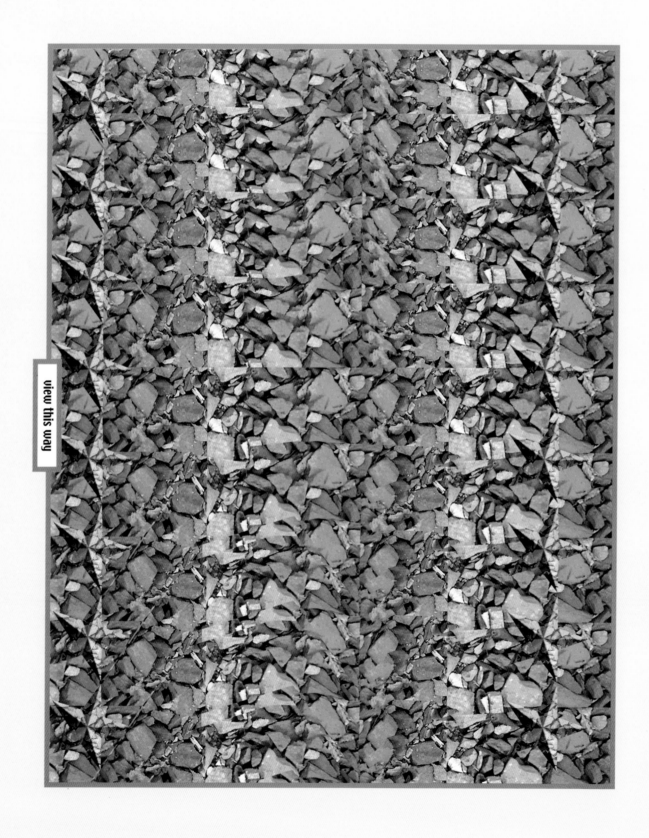

view this way

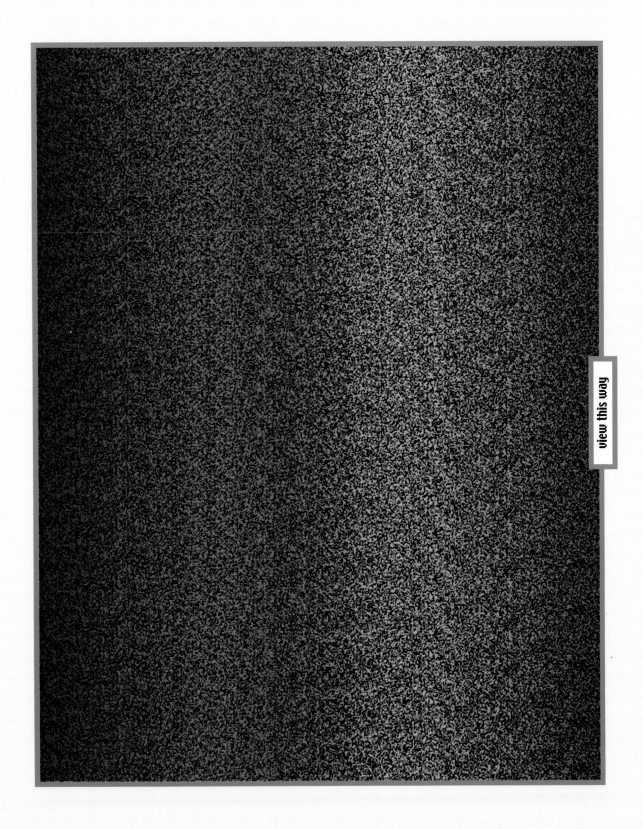

view this way

Piggy

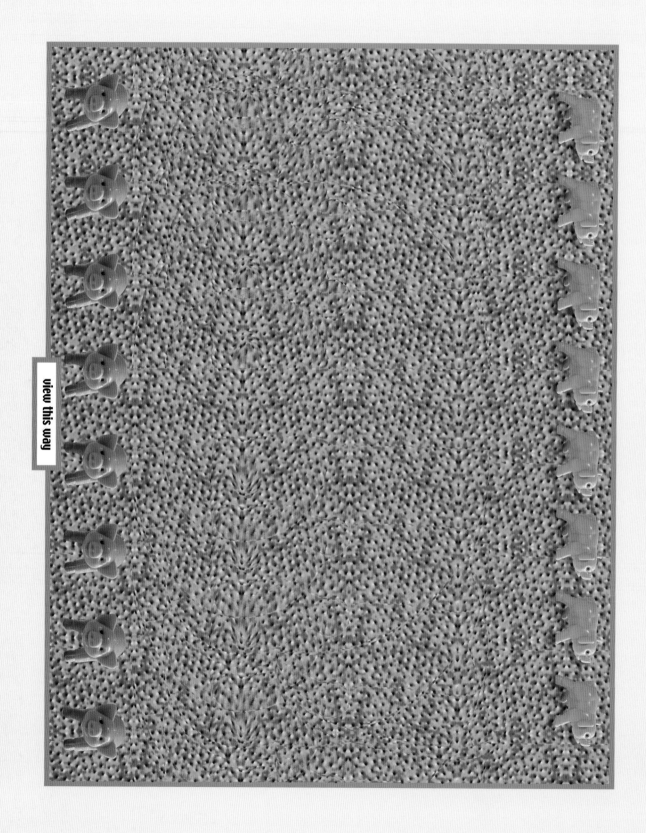

view this way

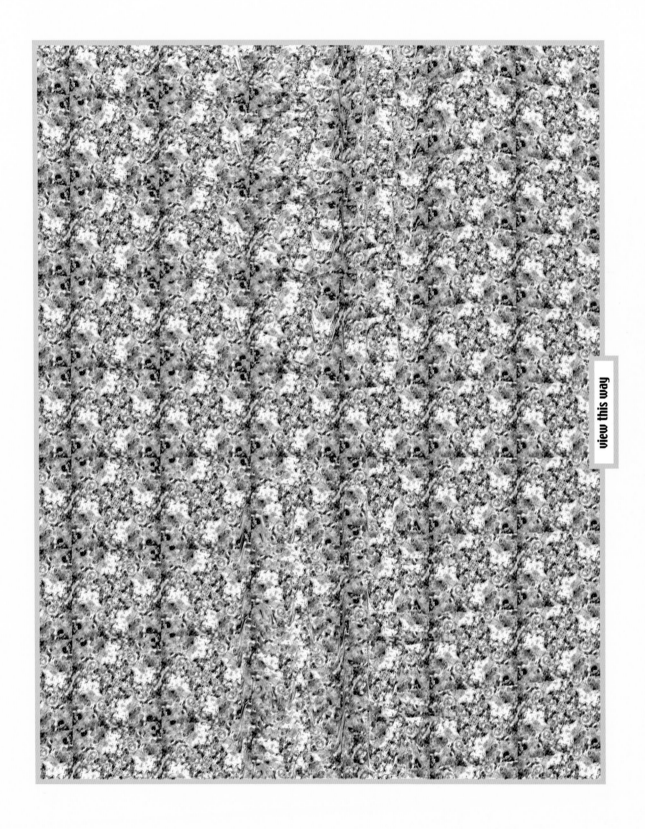

view this way

Susan's Basket

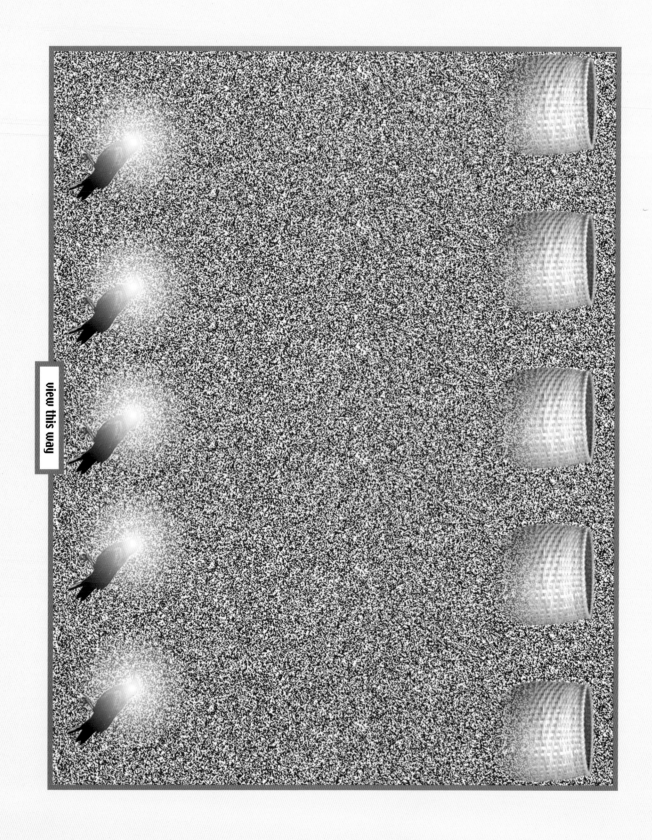

view this way

Susan's Basket

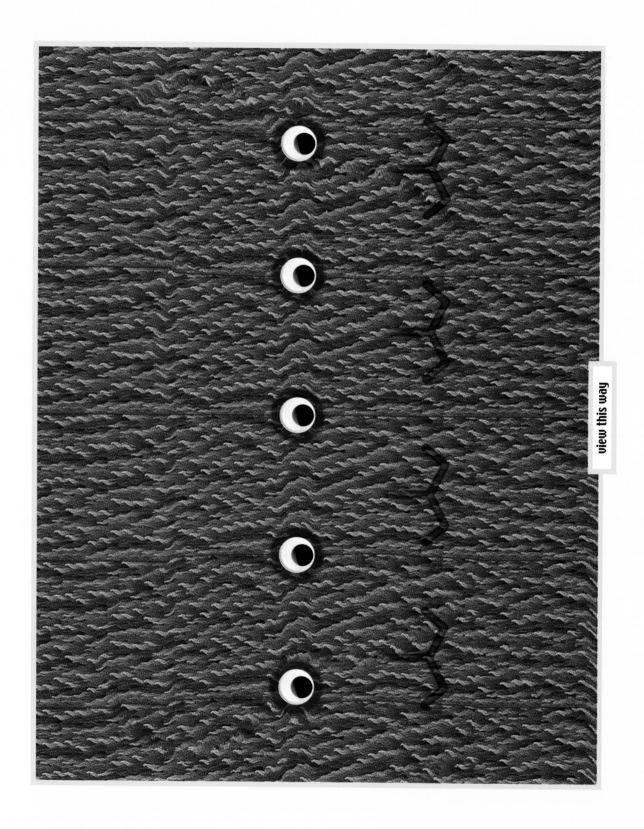

view this way

view this way

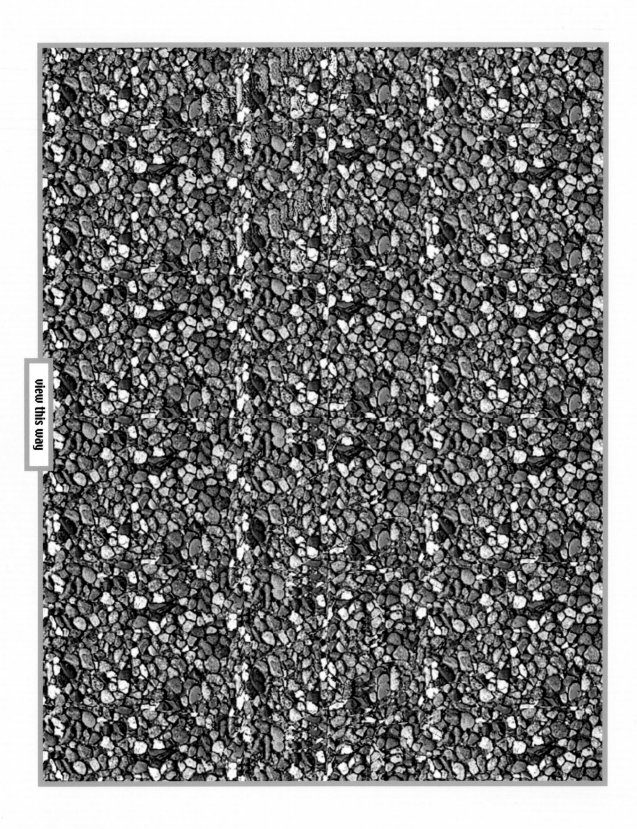

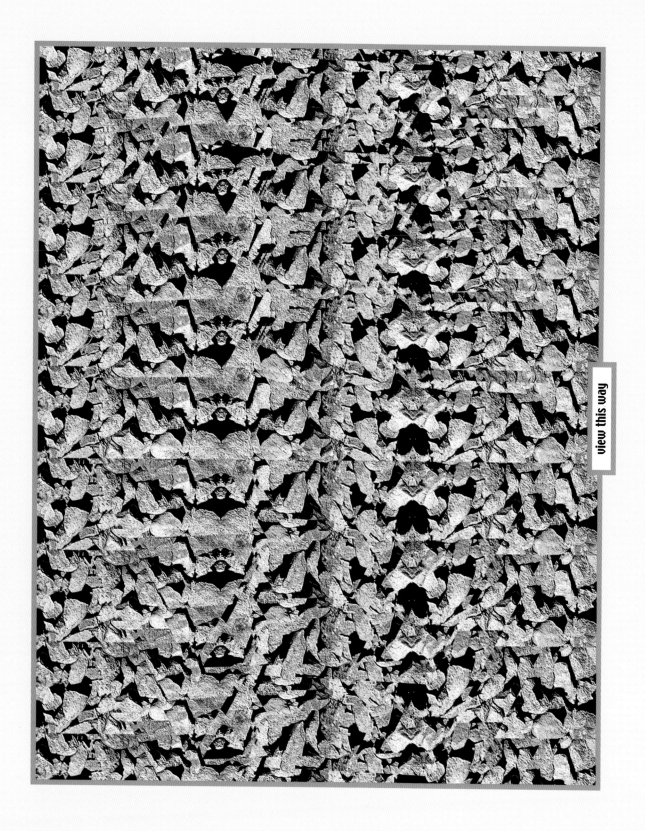

view this way

Cross Plus

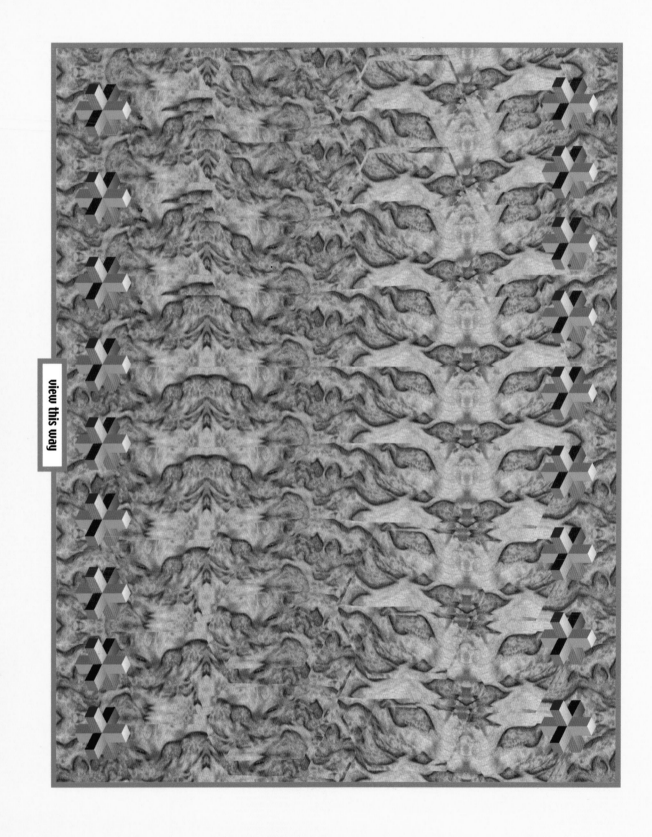

view this way

view this way

Lizard Bowls

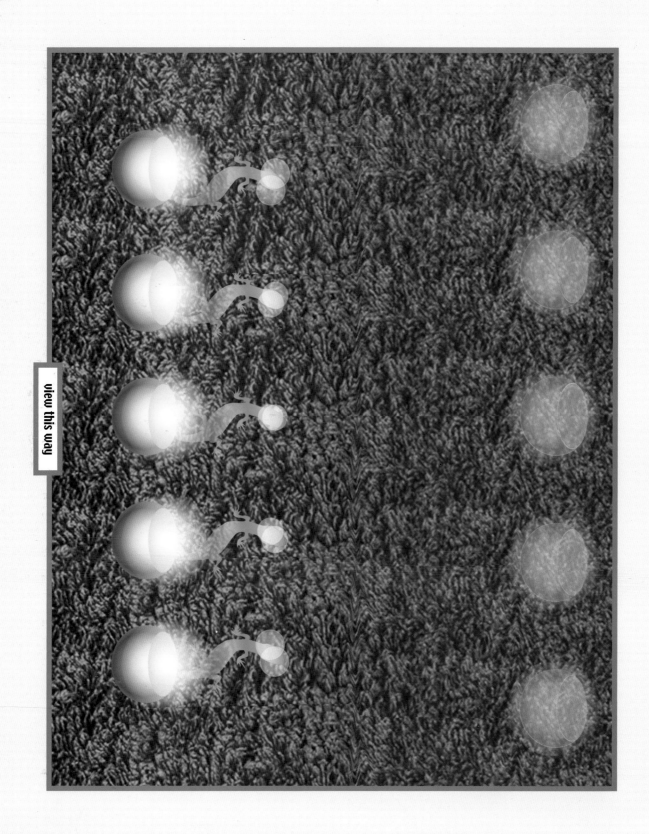

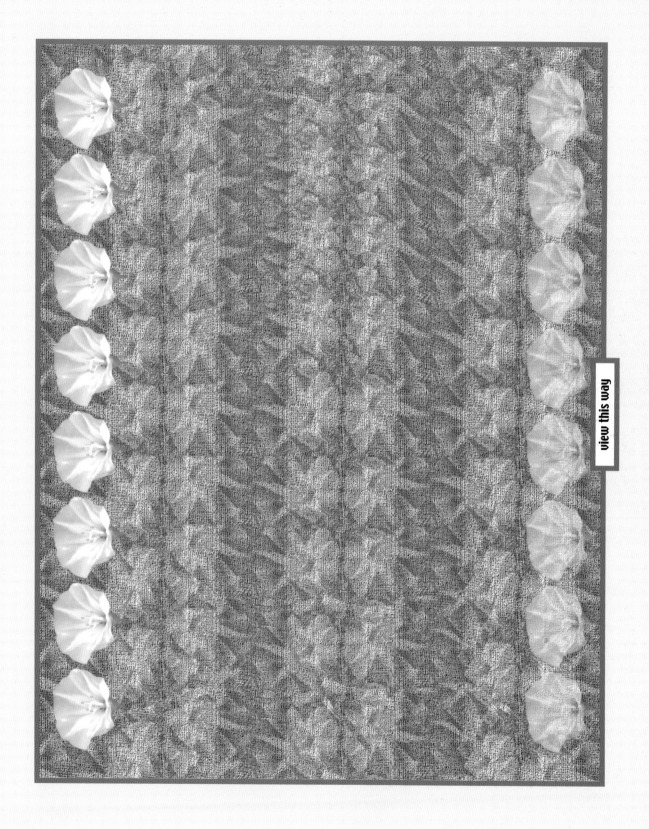

Oak Leaves

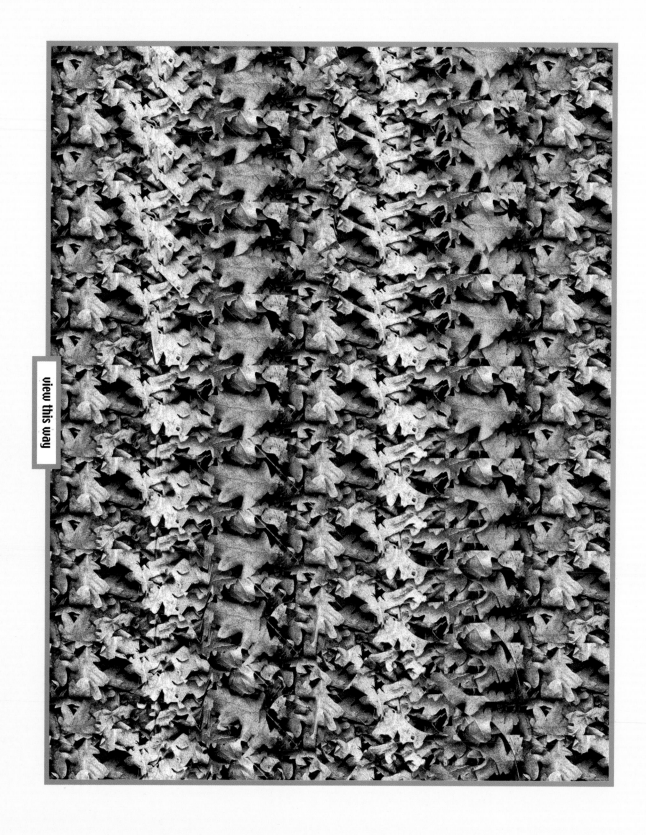

view this way

136

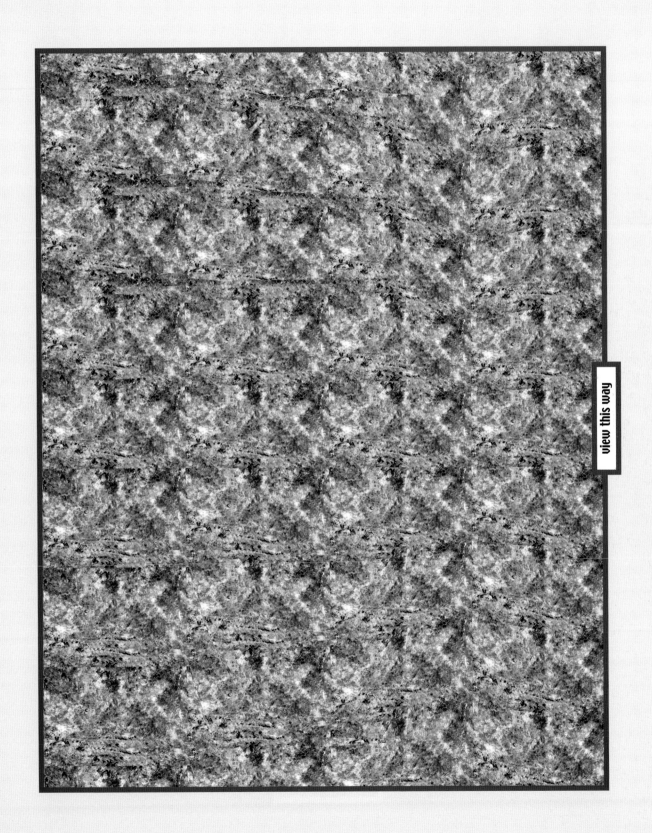

view this way

Pool Balls

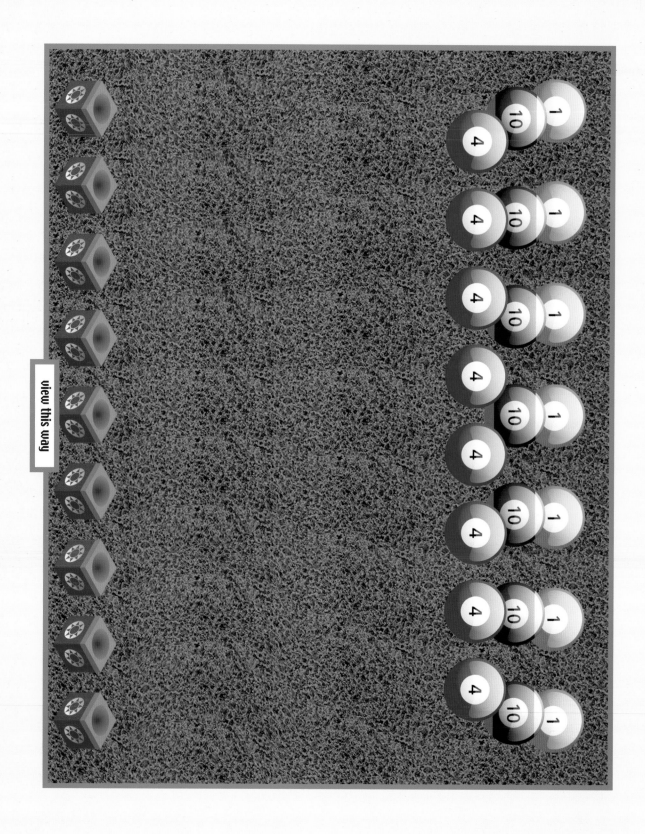

view this way

view this way

New Mexico

view this way

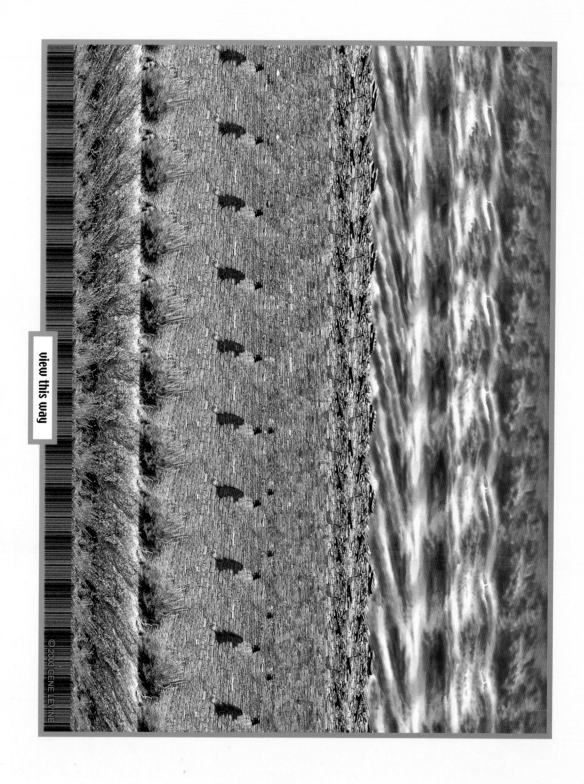

© 2003 GENE LEVINE

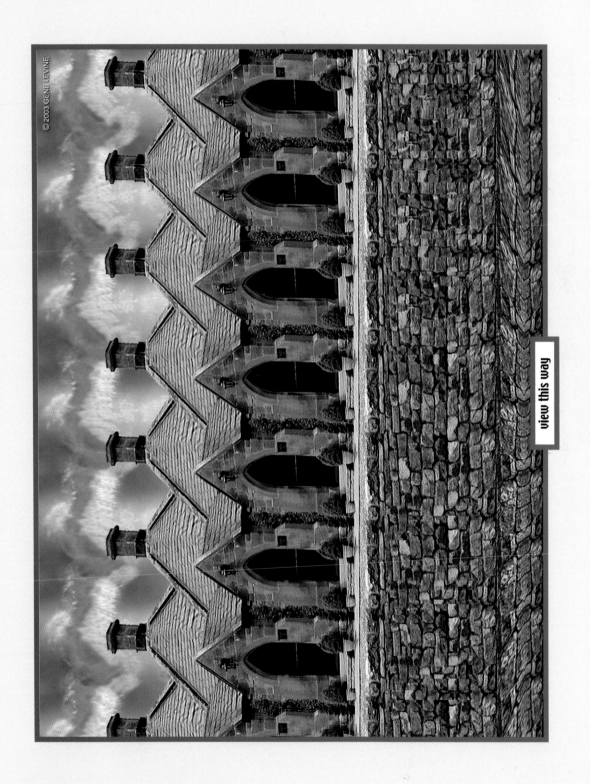

© 2003 GENE LEVINE

view this way

Organic Vacuum

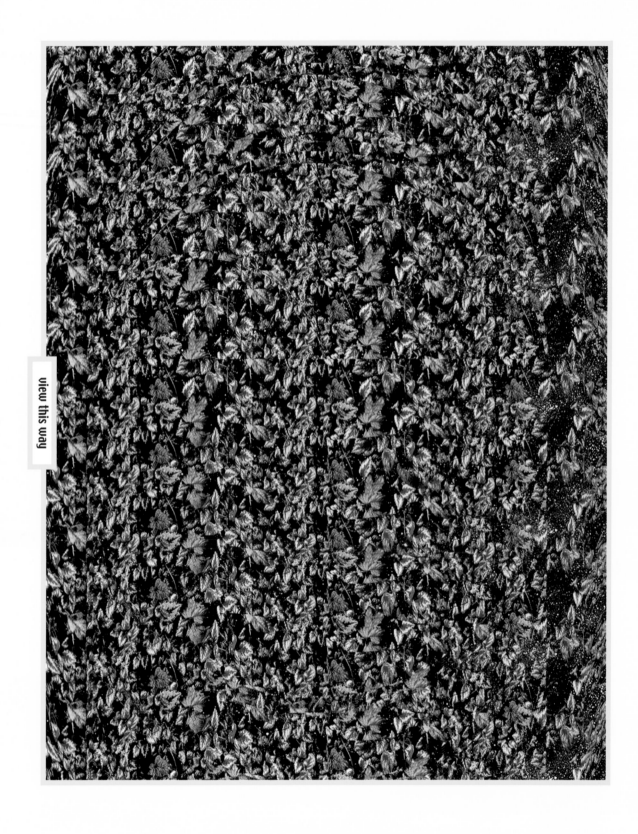

view this way

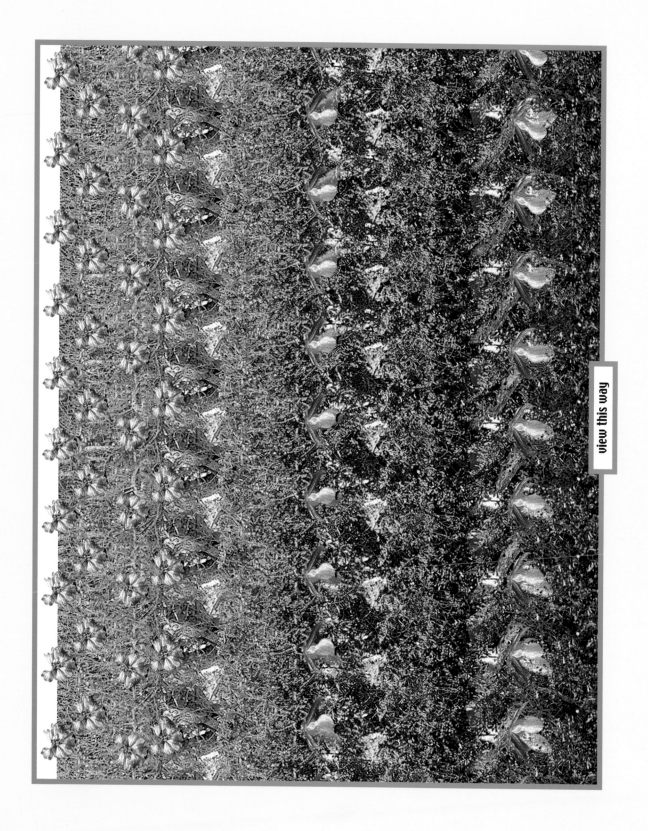

view this way

view this way

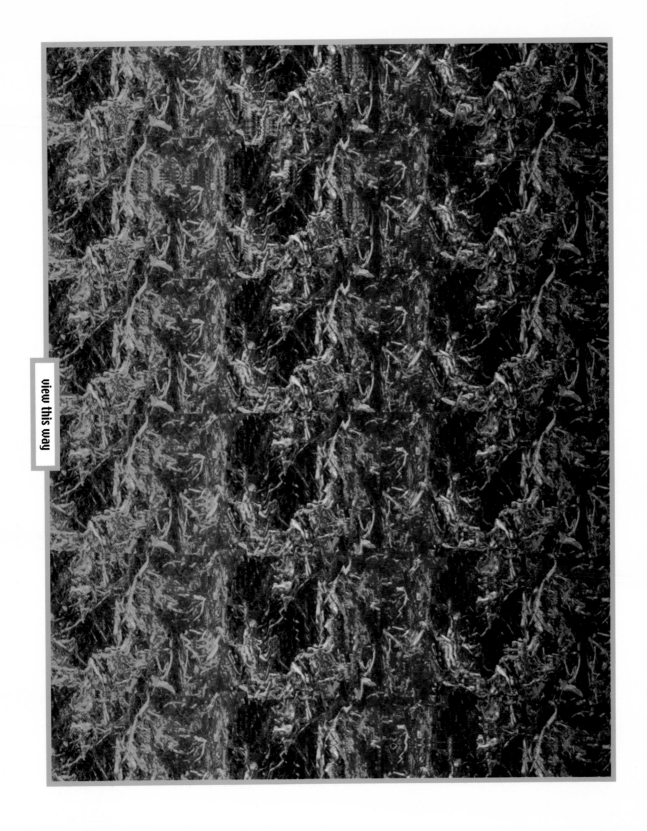

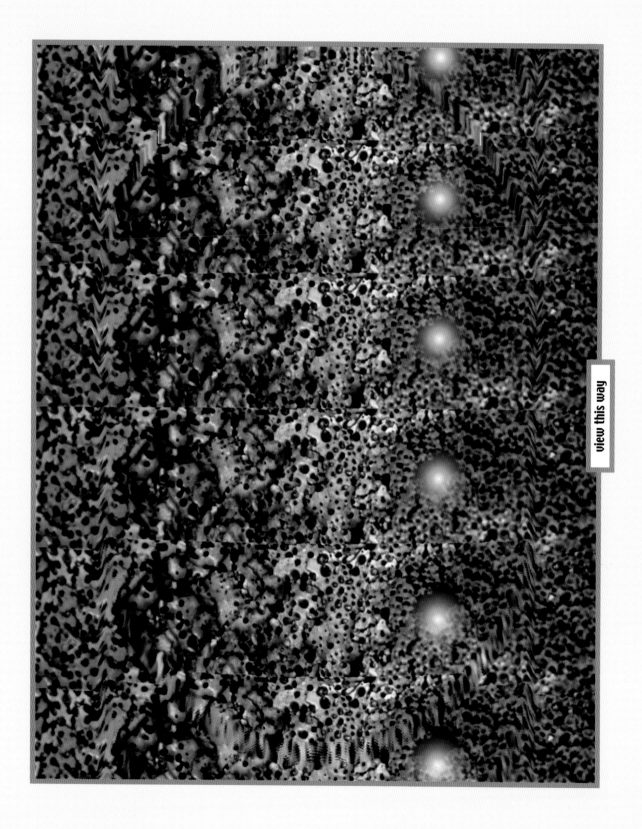

view this way

Abalone Shell

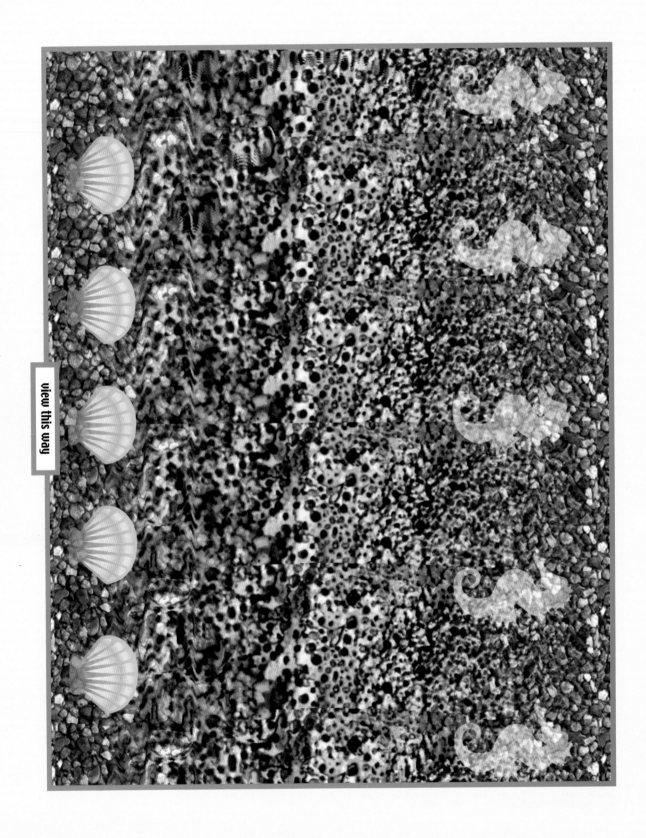

view this way

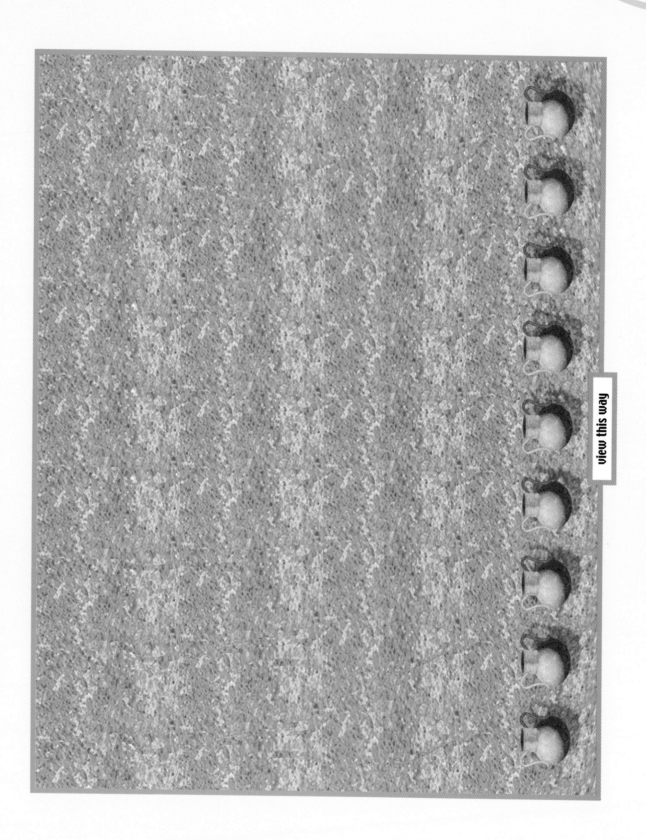

view this way

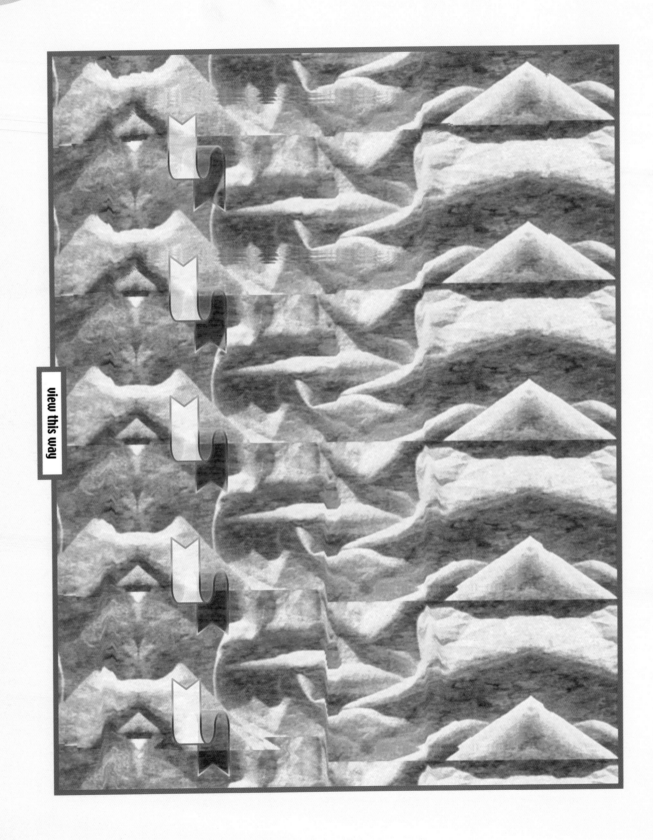

view this way

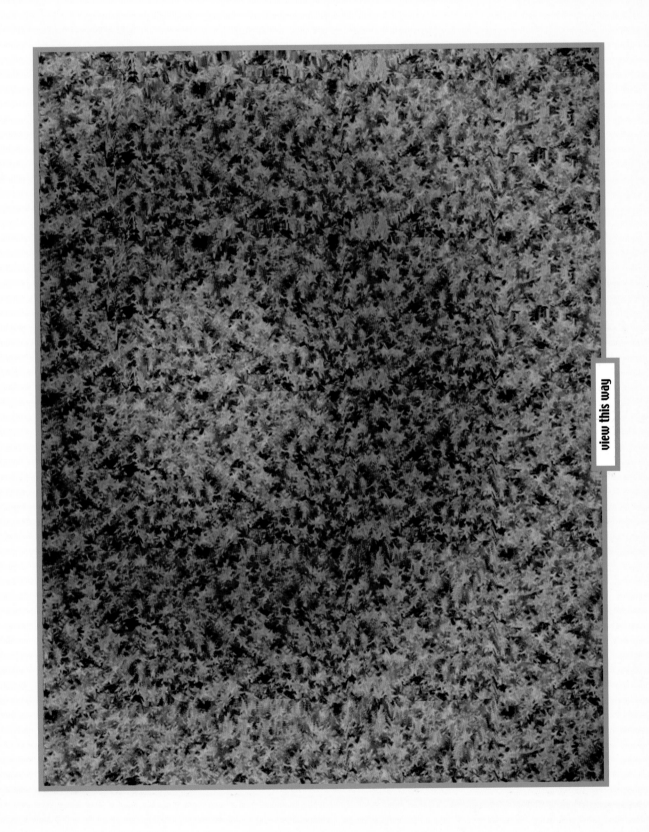

view this way

Building Blocks

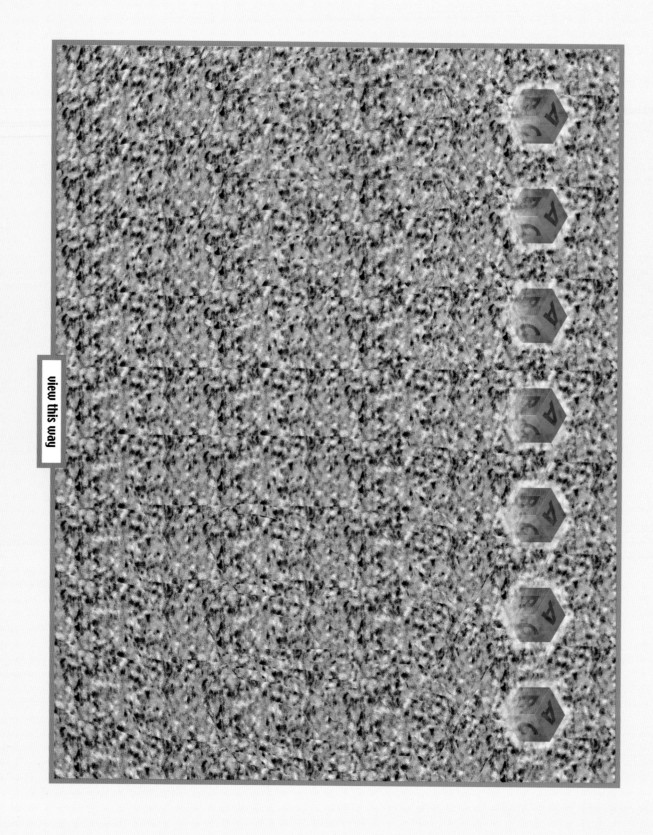

view this way

CELADON

view this way

Chrome Capsule

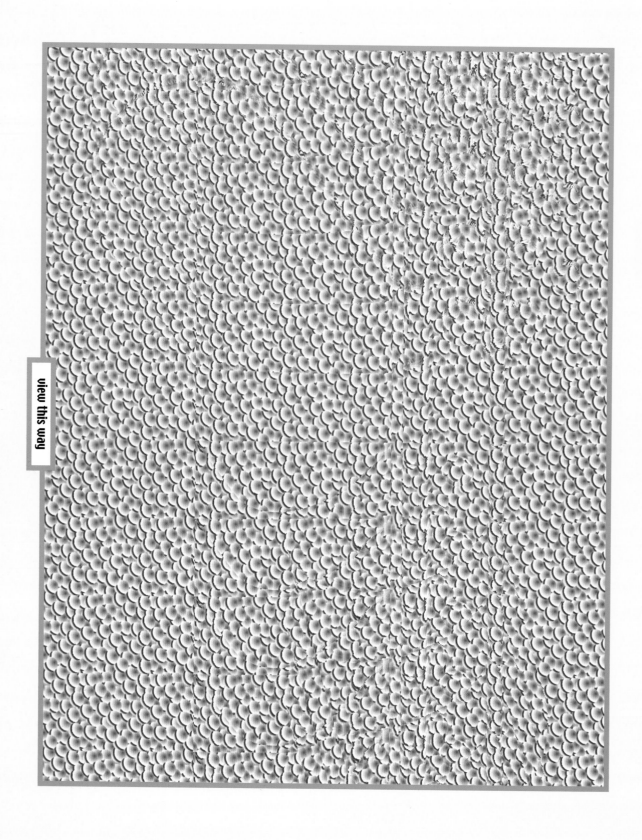

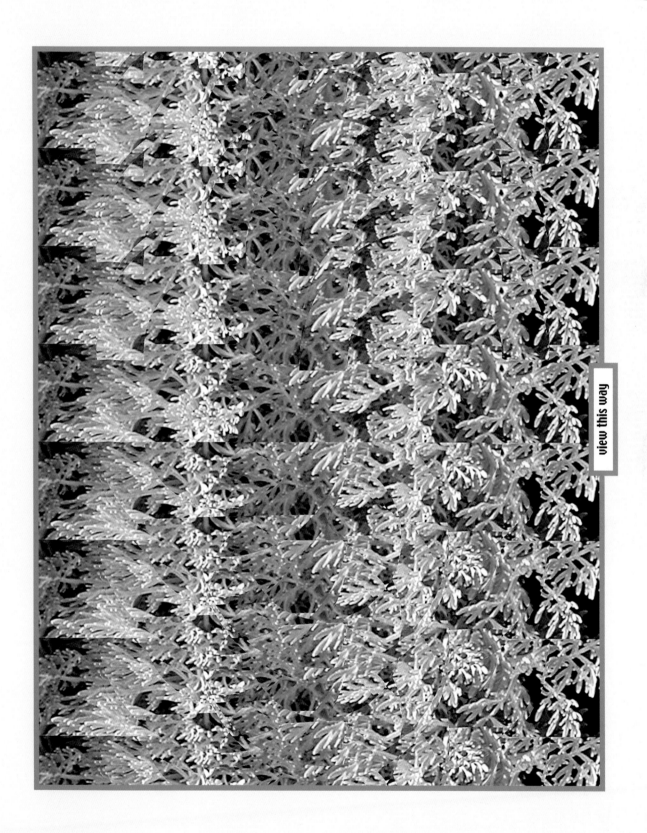

view this way

Dangerous Sea

view this way

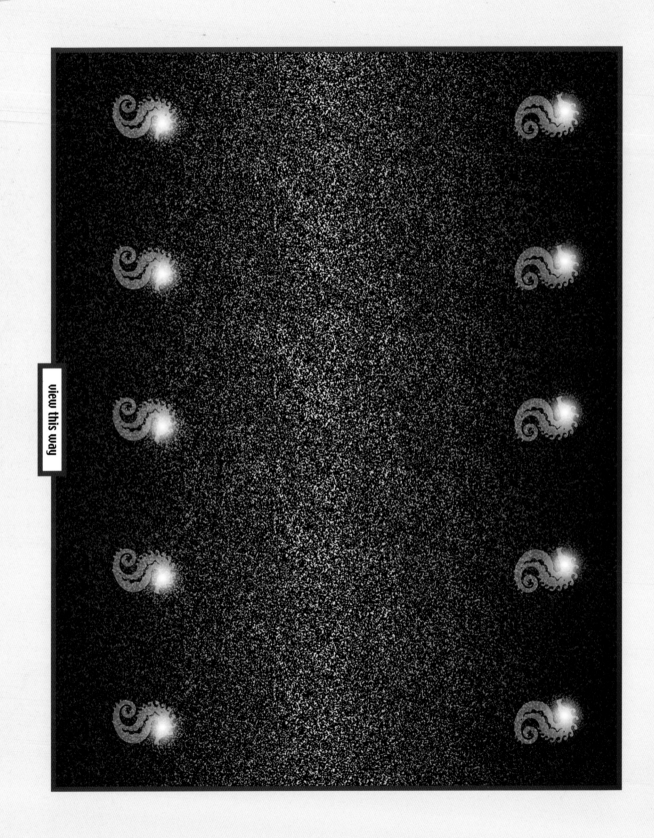

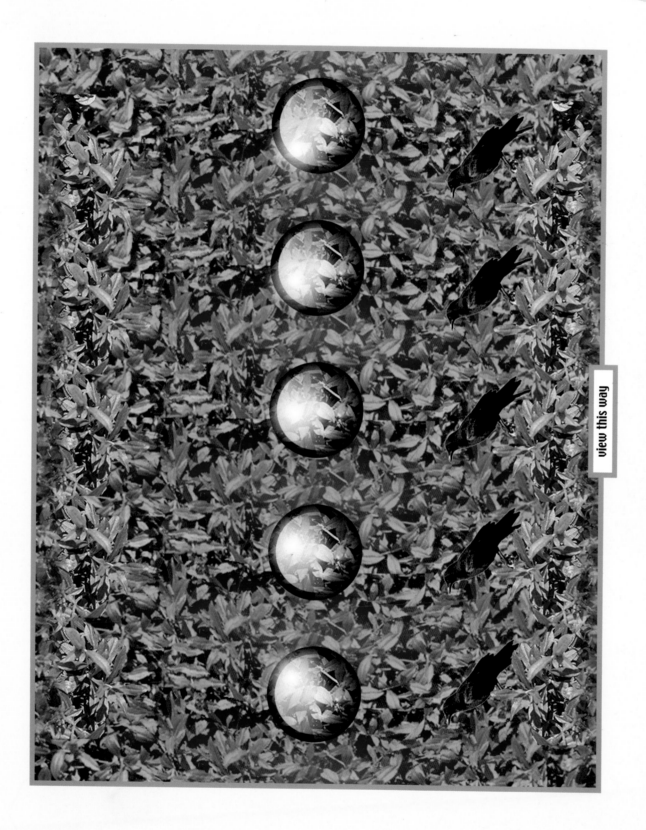

view this way

Desert Pyramid

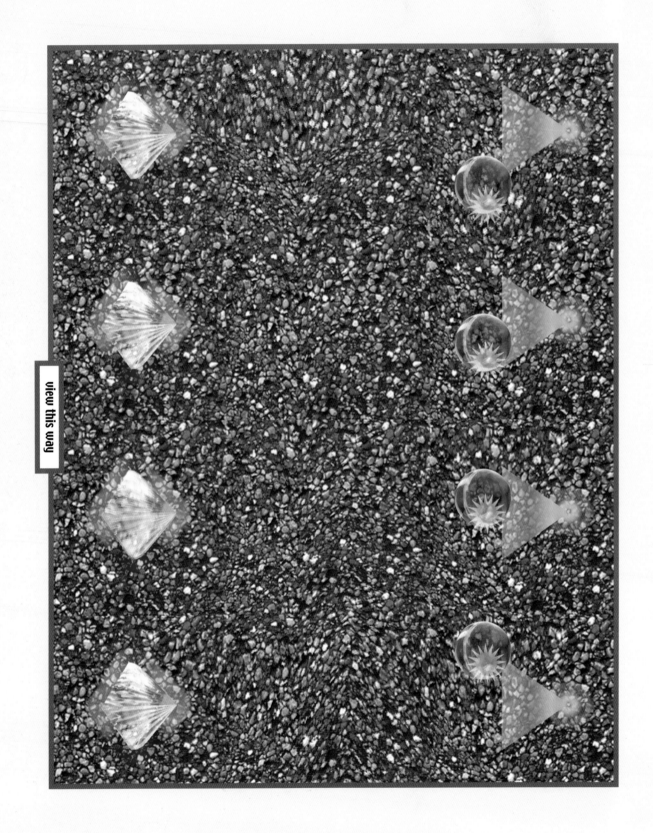

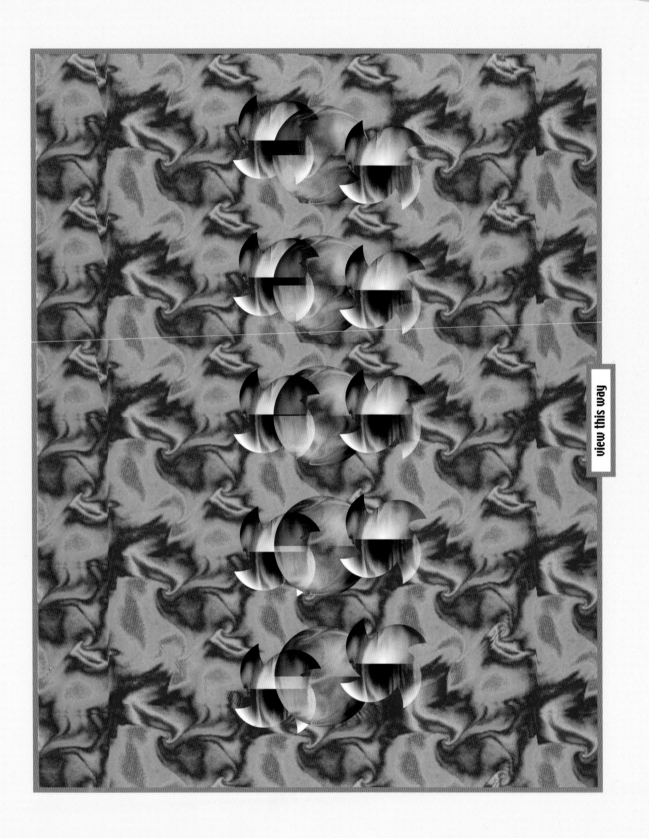

view this way

Eye of the Storm

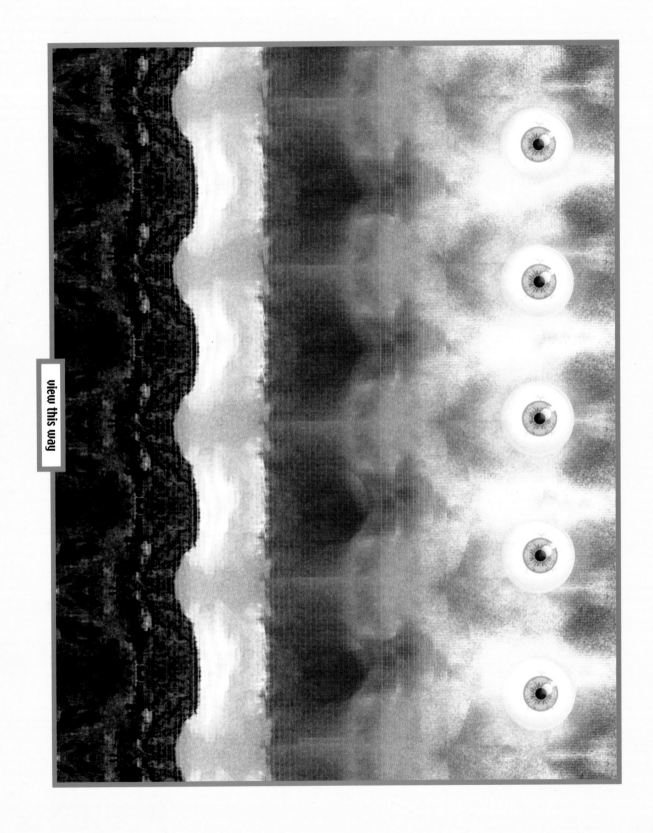

view this way

view this way

Interlocking Rings

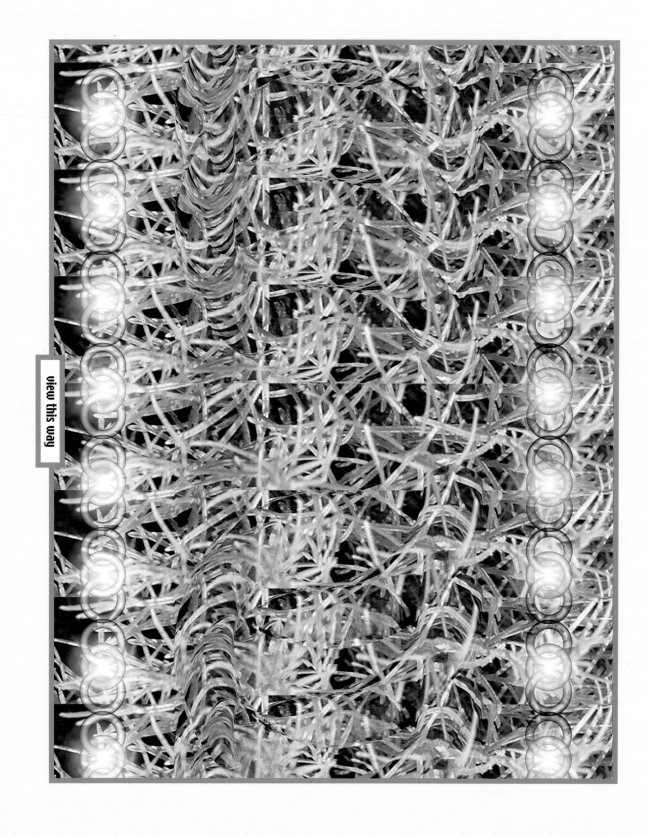

view this way

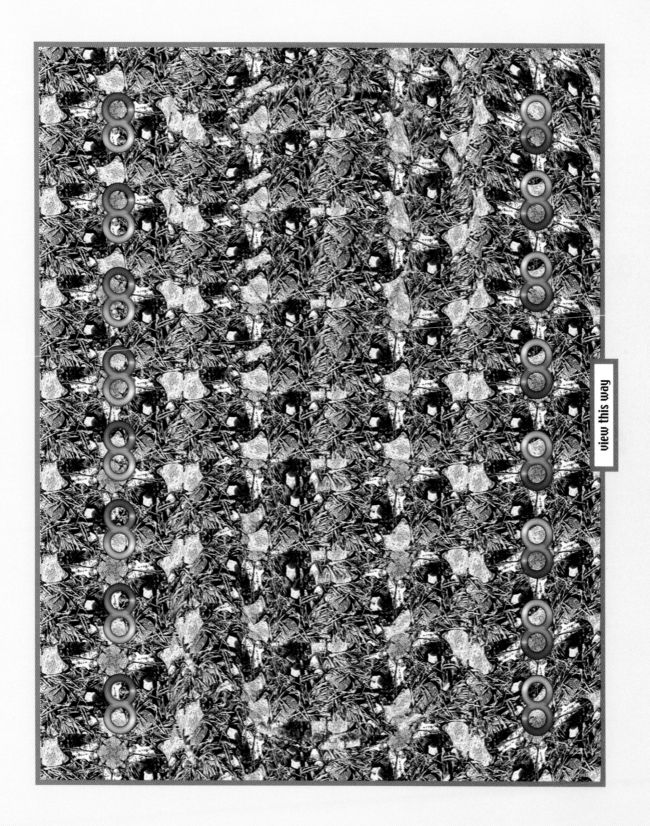

view this way

Happy Face

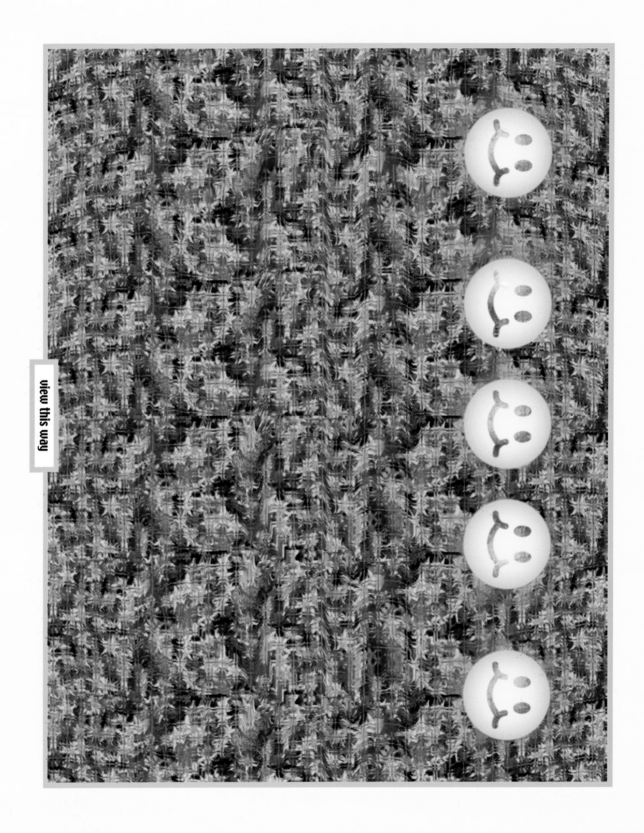

view this way

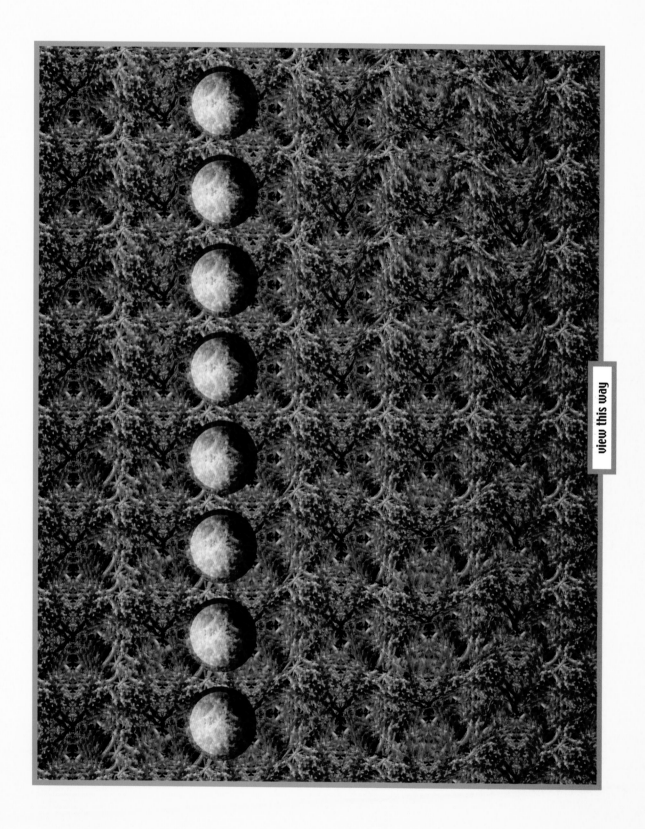

view this way

Ivy Cube

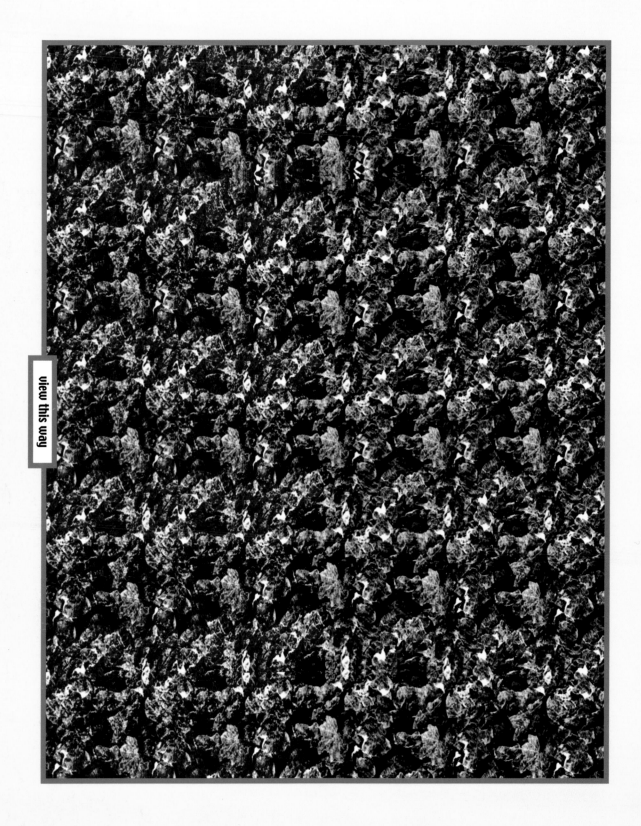

view this way

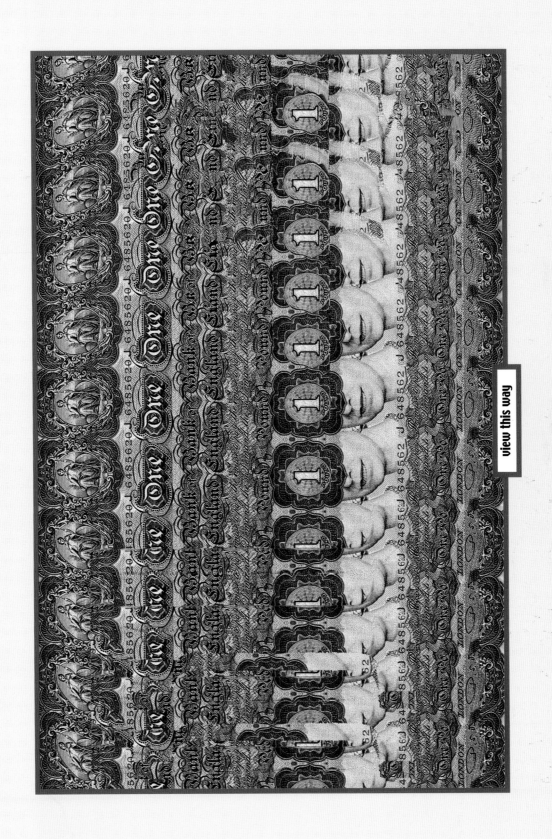

view this way

Stereosaurs

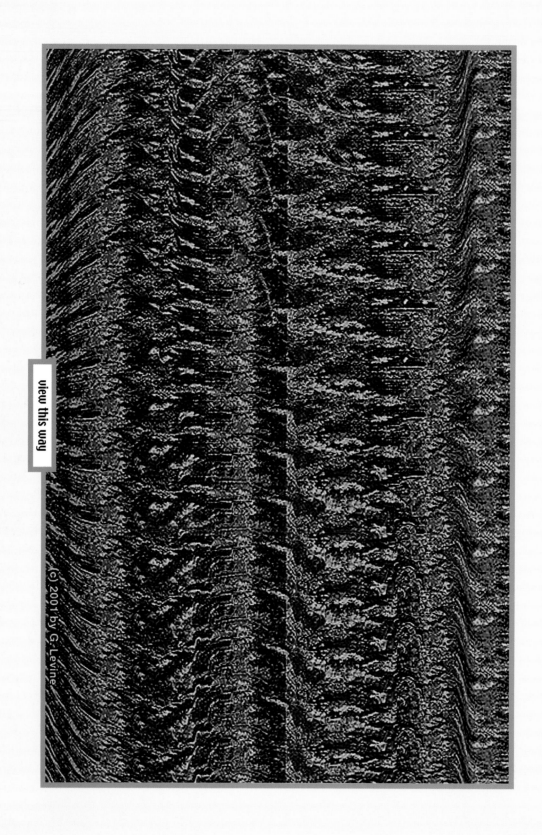

view this way

(c) 2001 by G. Levine

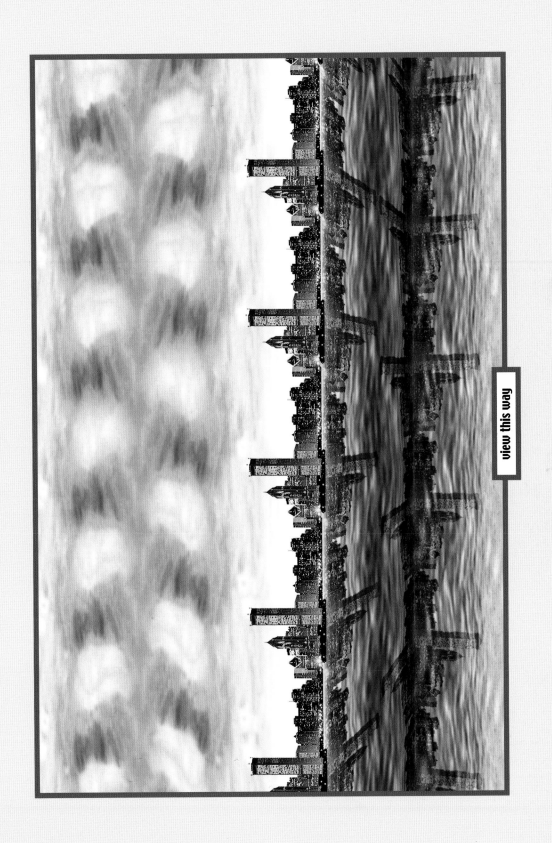

view this way

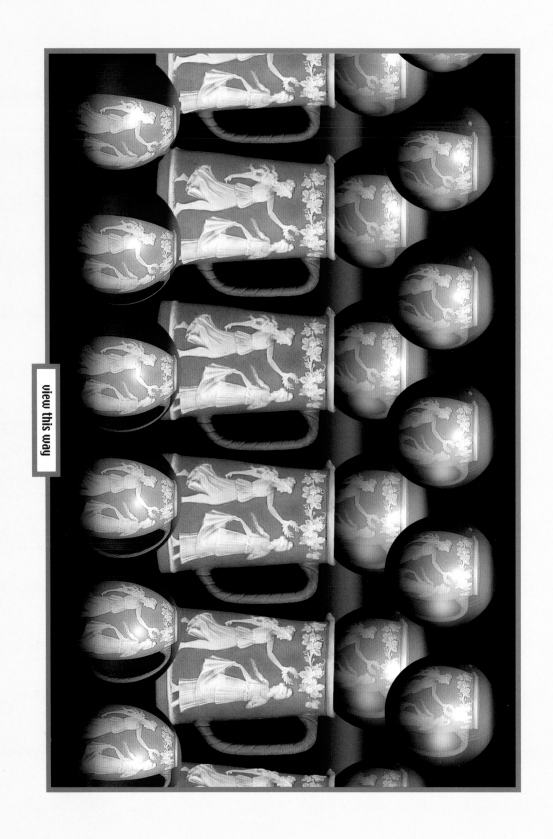

view this way

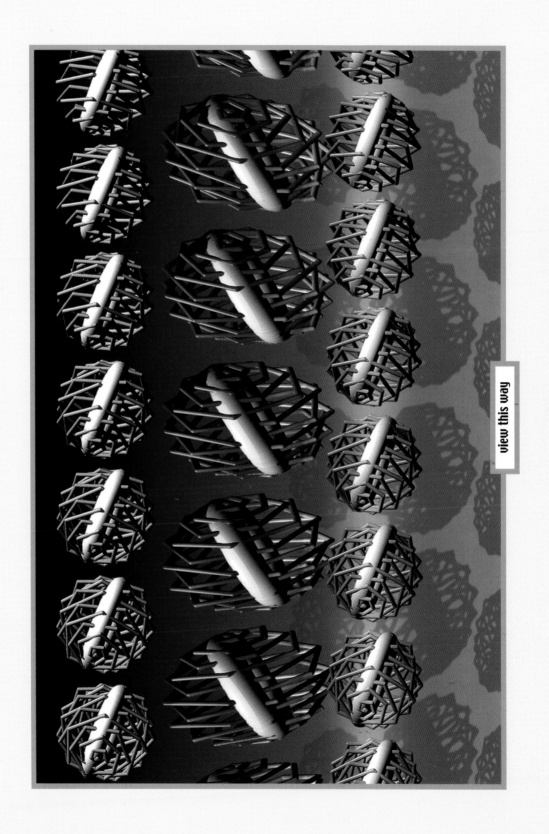

view this way

Kaleidoscopic Spiral

view this way

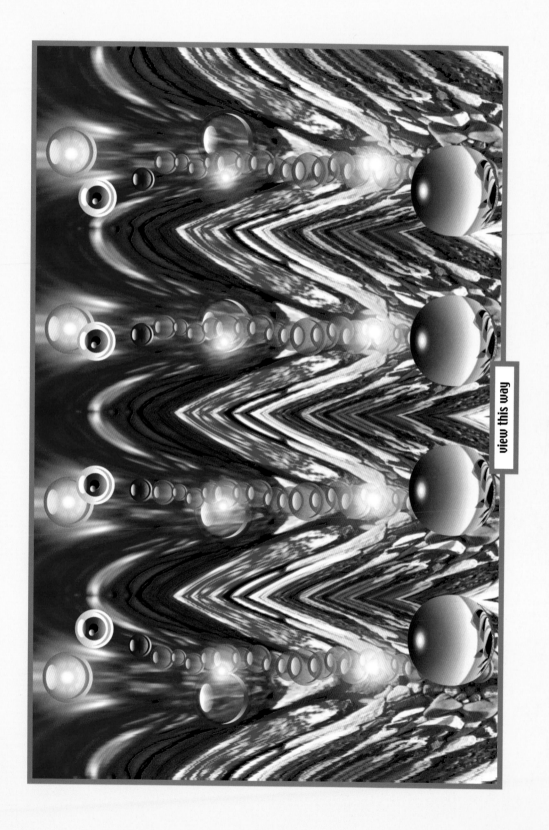

view this way

Granite Fu

view this way

view this way

(C) 1998 G Levine

French Chow

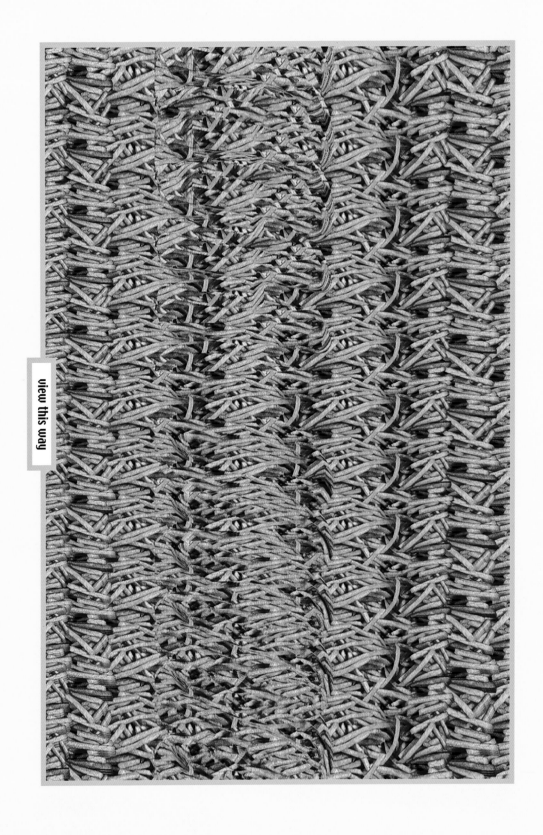

view this way

view this way

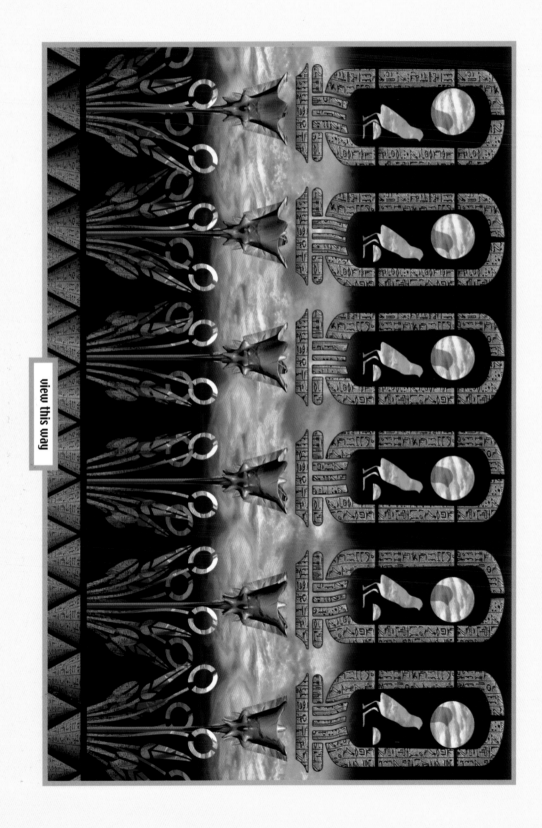

view this way

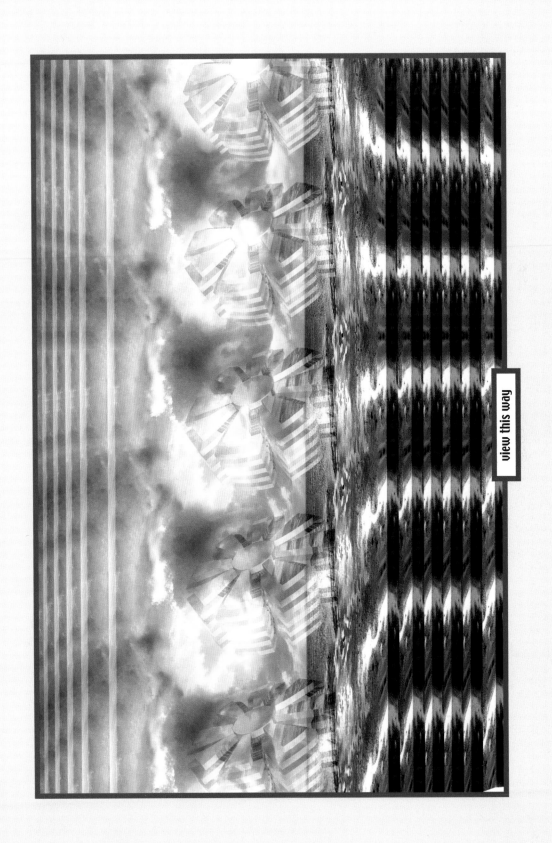

view this way

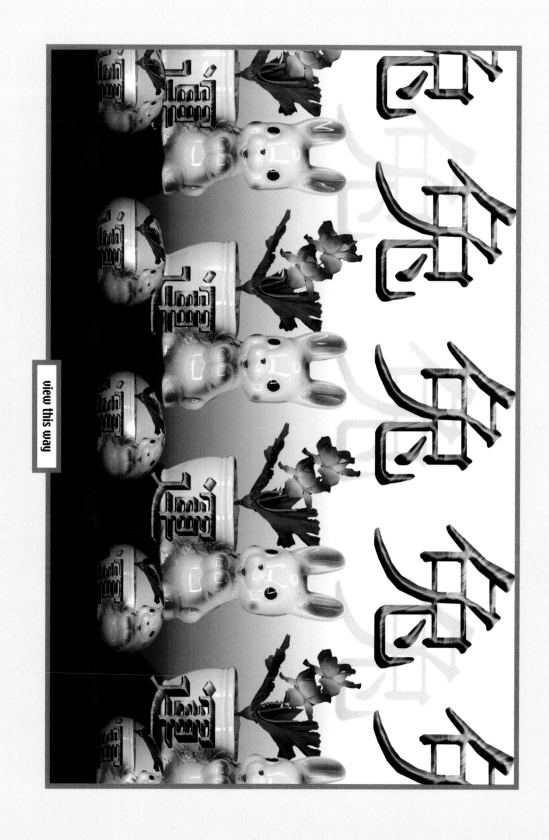

view this way

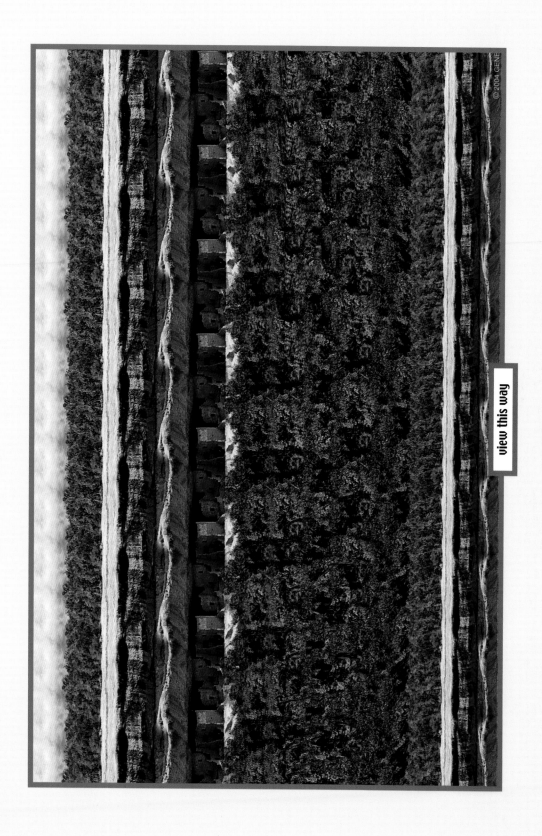

view this way

view this way

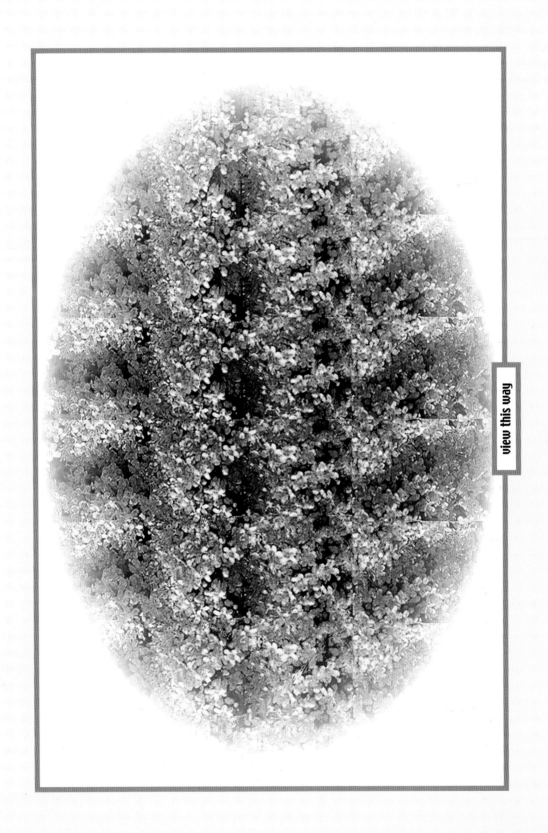

view this way

Sea Palace

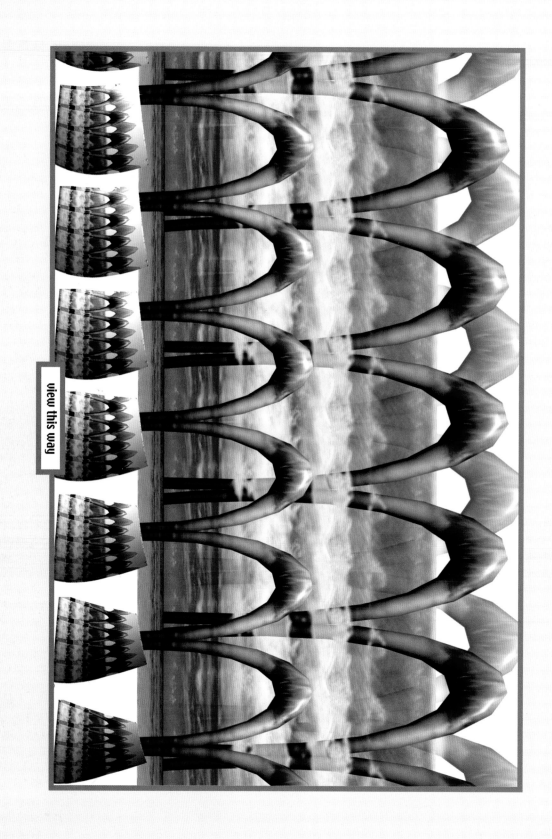

view this way

view this way

Inspiration

view this way

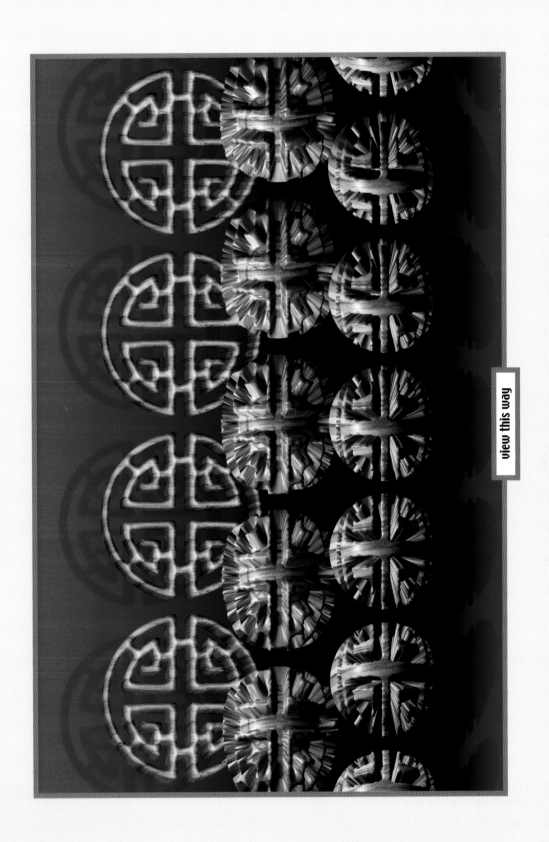

view this way

Lotus Garden

view this way

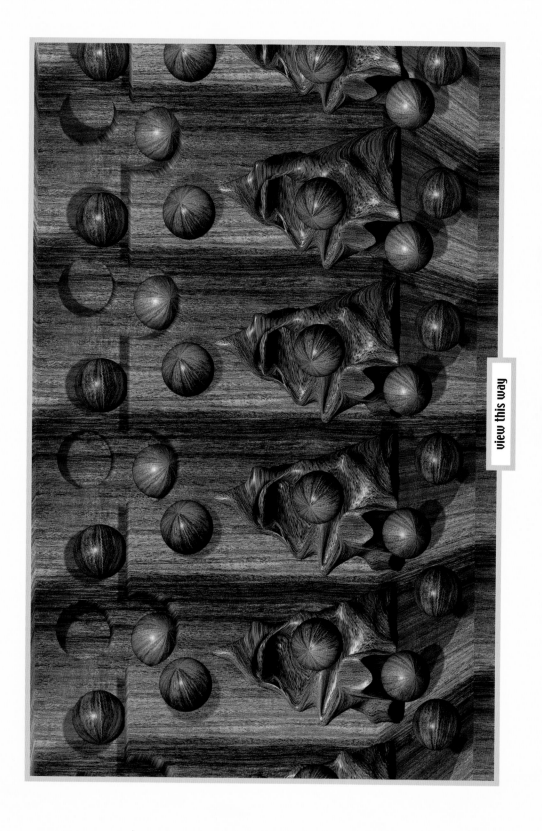

view this way

Floating Eyes

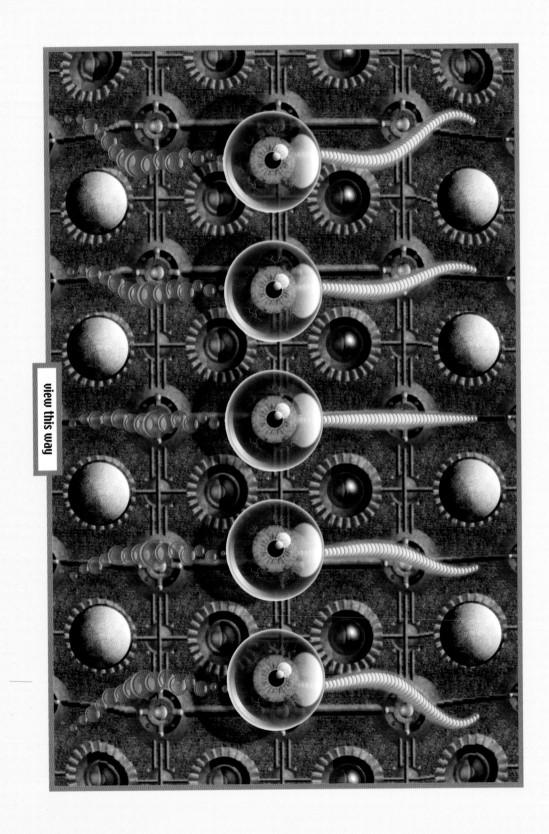

view this way

view this way

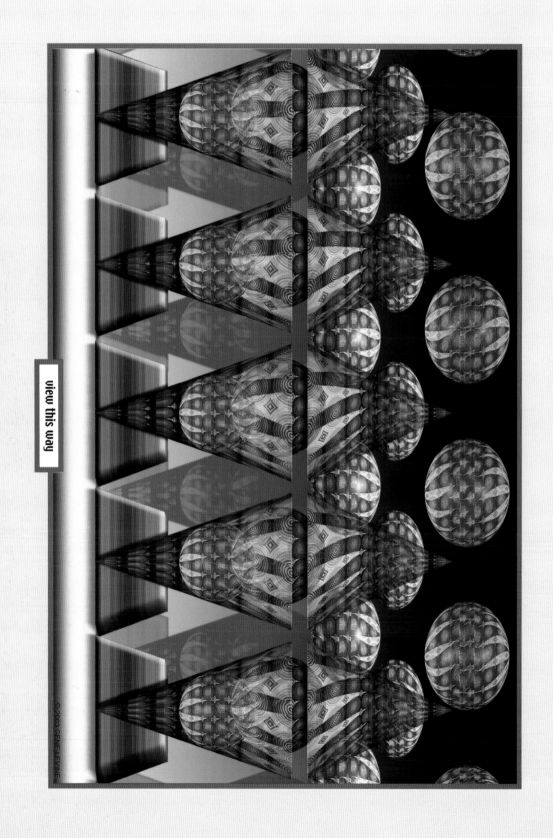

view this way

© 2003 GENE LEVINE

view this way

Rose Rows

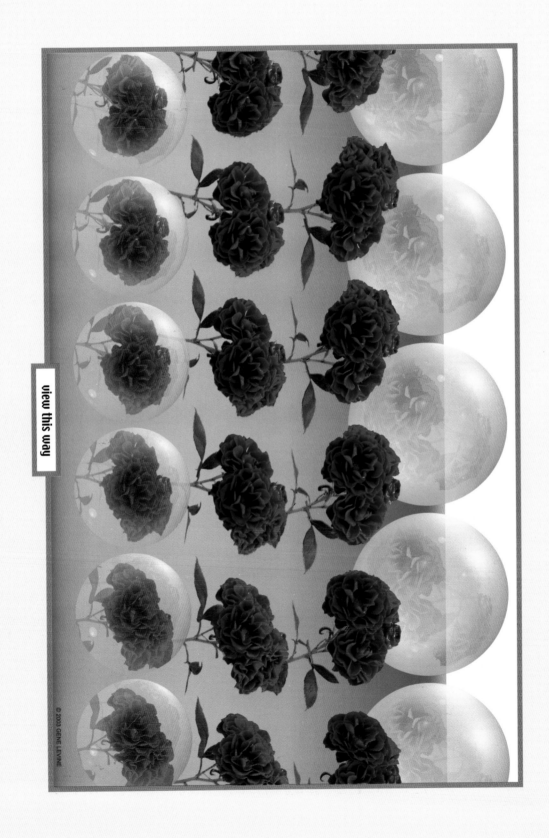

view this way

© 2003 GENE LEVINE

view this way

view this way

view this way

Blue Butterfly

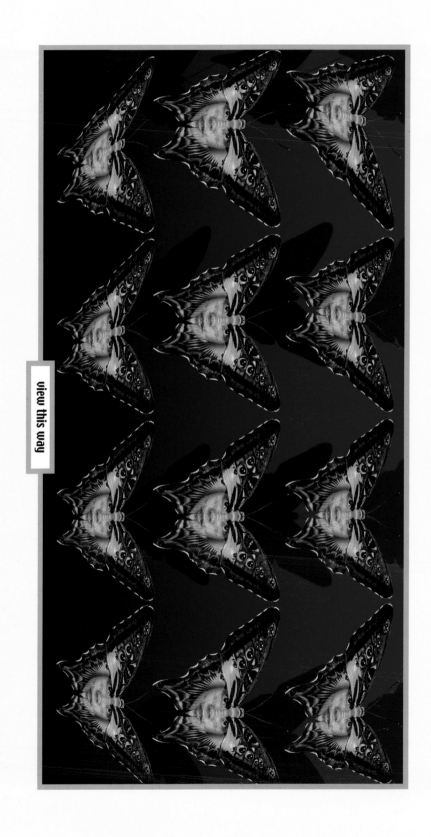

view this way

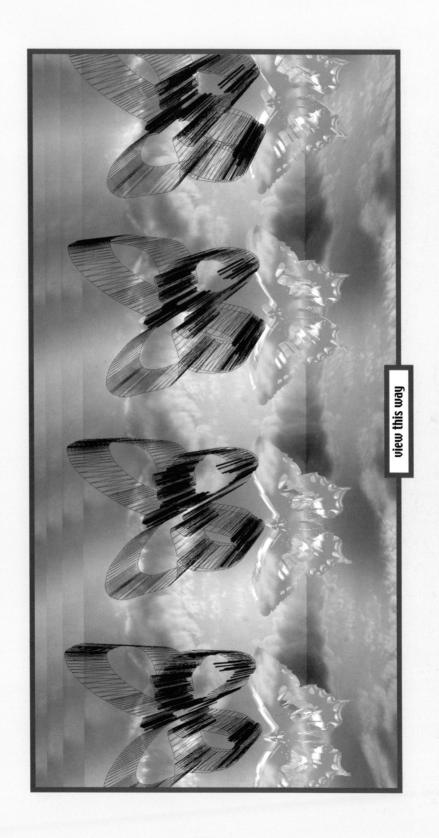

view this way

Butterfly Scarf

view this way

© 2002 GENE LEVII

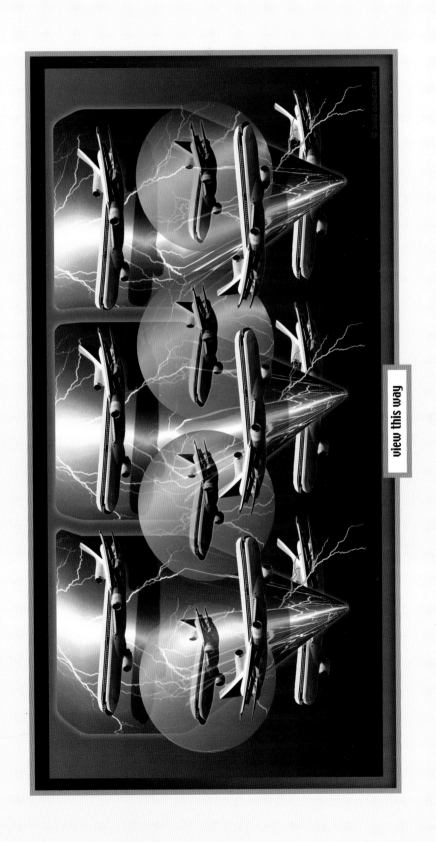

view this way

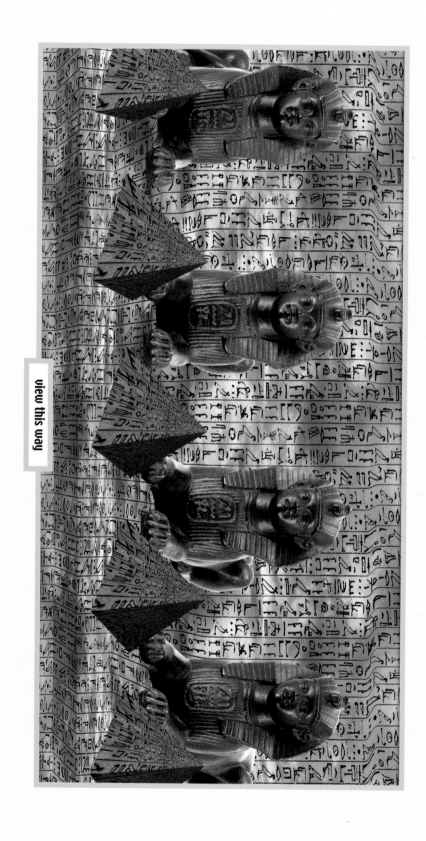

view this way

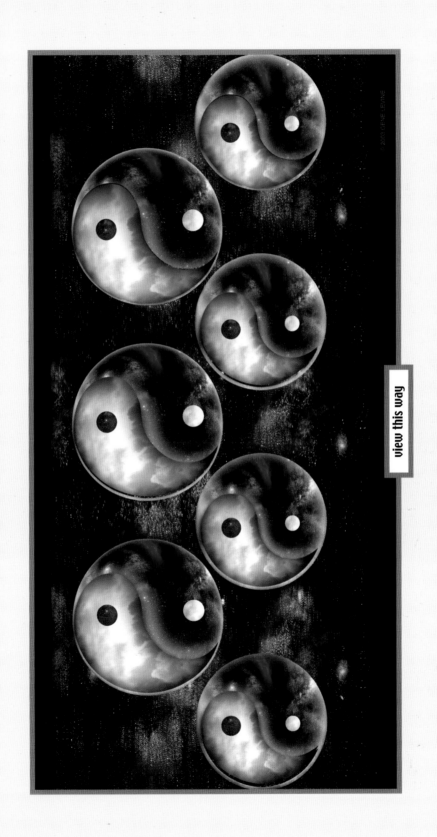

view this way

Swimming Ocean

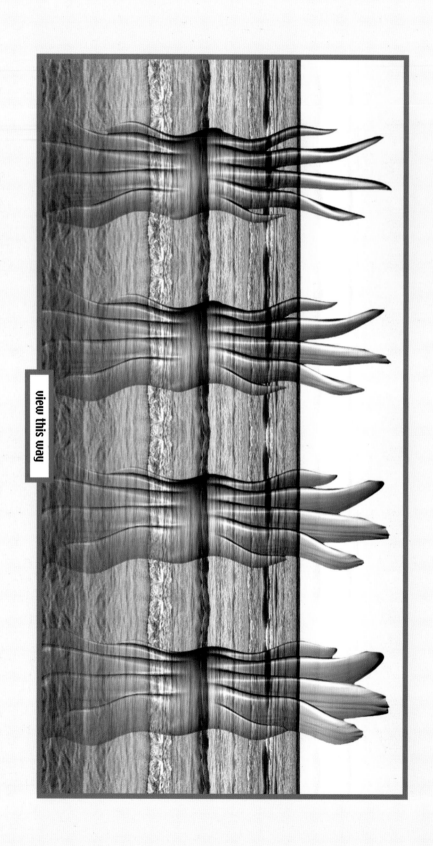

view this way

202

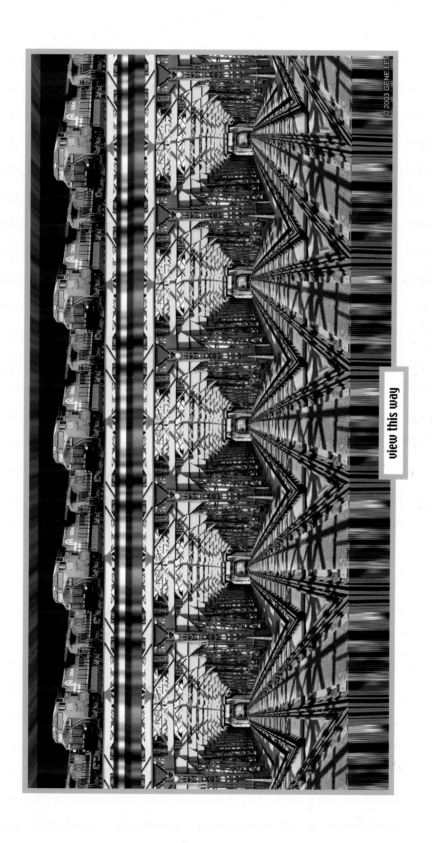

view this way

© 2003 GENE LEV

Sunset

view this way

204

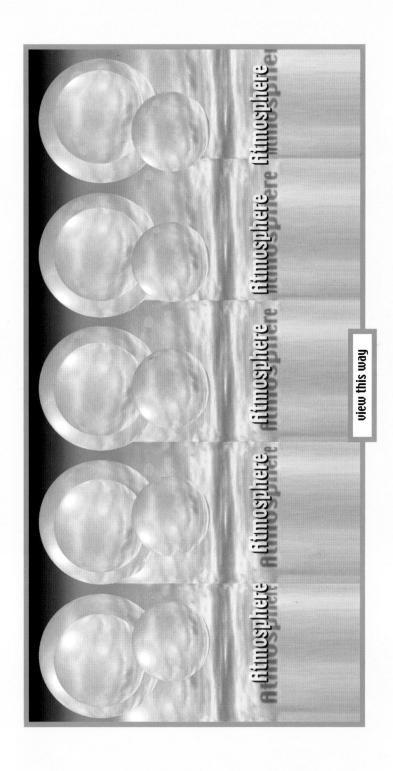

view this way

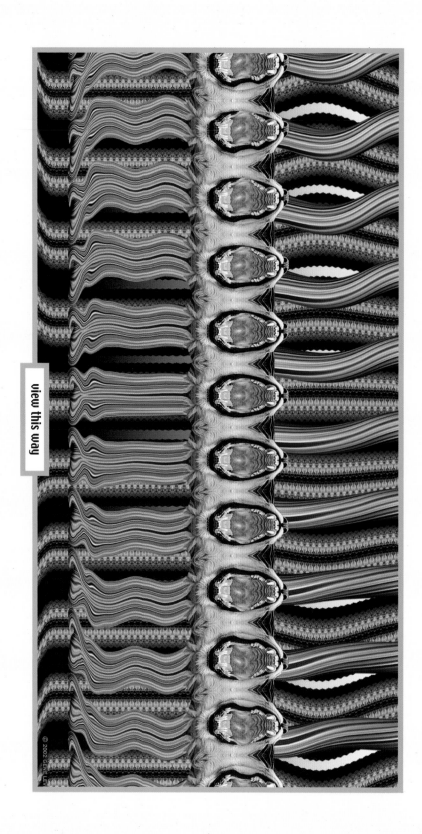

view this way

© 2002 GENE LEV

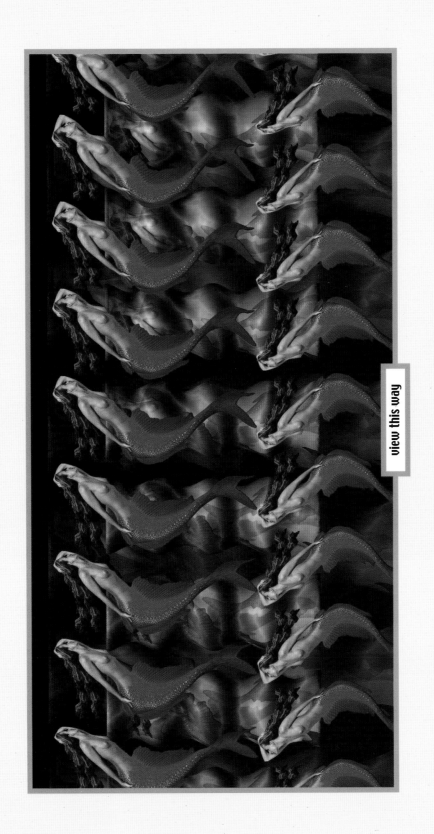

view this way

Revelations

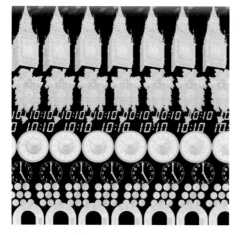

page 8   Stereo Time

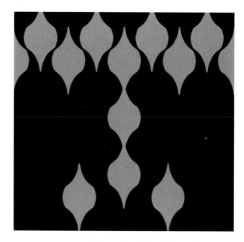

page 9   Aster Turf

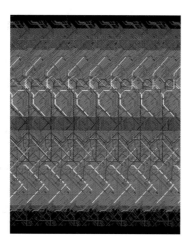

page 10   London Disconnect

page 11   Shamrocks

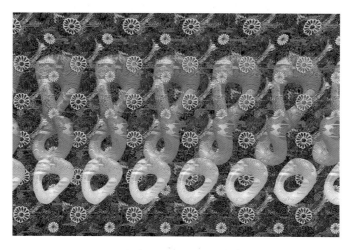

page 12   Blossom Waves

Revelations

page 13   Fruit Bat

page 14   Cherry Blossom

page 15   Crown Thee

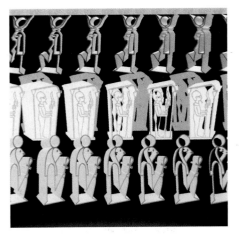

page 16   Egyptian Shadows

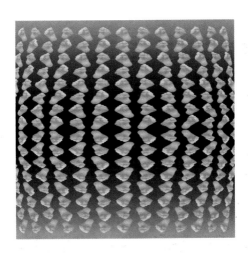

page 17   Footsteps

Revelations

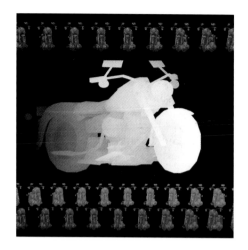

page 18   Stereocycle

page 19   Sundial

page 20   Lake View

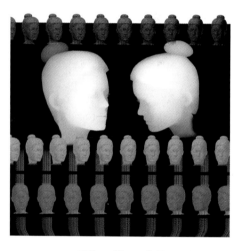

page 21   Head Bands

page 22   Wing Wang

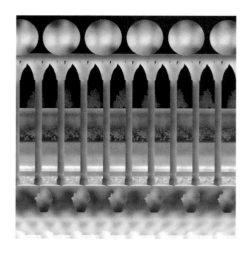

page 23   The Yard

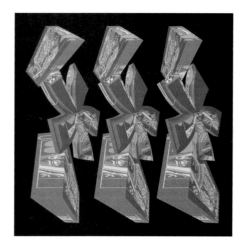

page 24   King & Queen

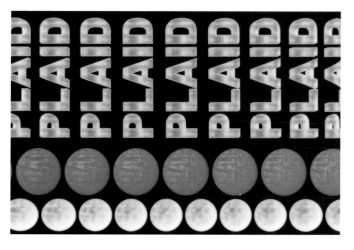

page 25   Glad Plaid

page 26   Point Burst

page 27   Flowers with a Twist

Revelations

page 28 Diamonds in the Rough

page 29   Dragonfly Sparks

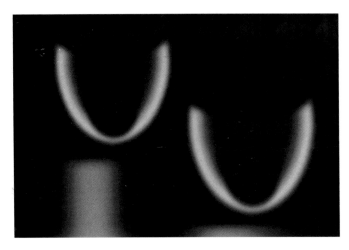

page 30 Johnny's Garden

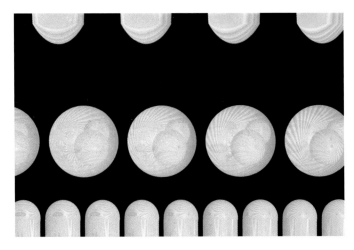

page 31   Frax Bubbles

page 32   Butterfly Pillows

Revelations

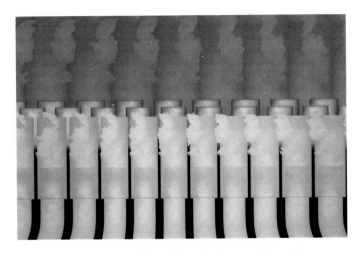

page 33   Cloud Funnels

page 34   Colour Sieve

page 35   Dragon Light

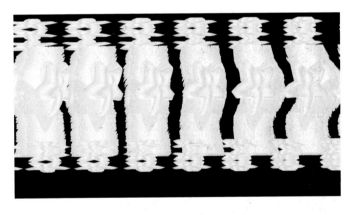

page 36   Molten Water

page 37   Mixed Vegetables

Revelations

page 38   Star Screen

page 39   Star Family

page 40   Man & Woman

page 41   Making Honey

page 42   Hidden Image

Revelations

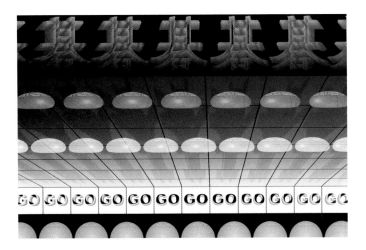

page 43   Go

page 44   Fireworks

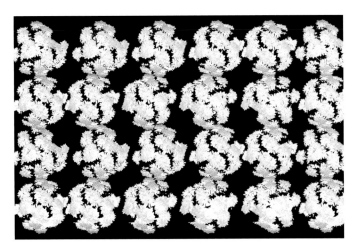

page 45   Floral Twists

page 46   Footprints

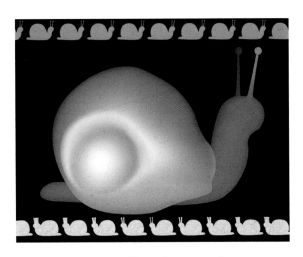

page 47   Escargot

Revelations

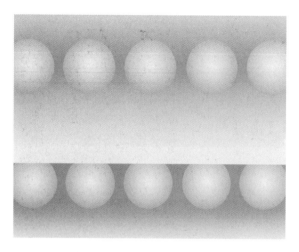

page 48   Gold Eye Sky

page 49   Goldfish

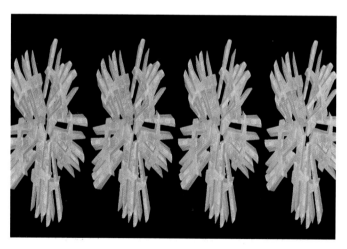

page 50   Stone Burst

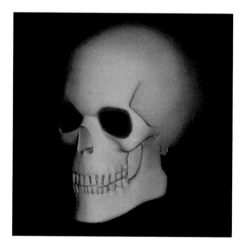

page 51   The Phrenologist

page 52   Takeoff & Landing

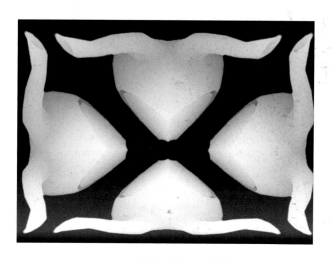

page 53   Temple Albathor

page 54   Heart in Heart

page 55   Heart-throb

Revelations

page 56   Terraced

page 57   The Guardian

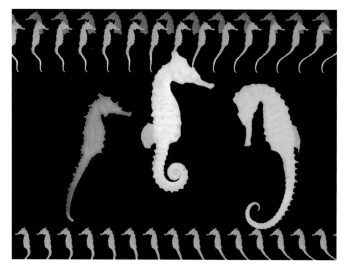

page 58   Seahorse Herd

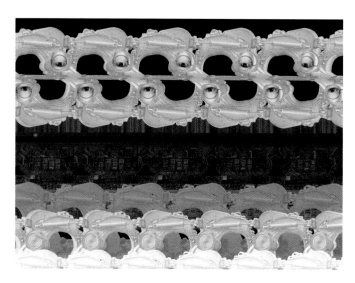

page 59   The Stereogram Machine

page 60   Box in a Box

page 61   Butterfly

page 62   Celtic Knot

page 63   Comedy

Revelations

page 64   Dice

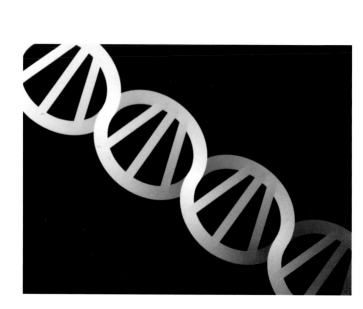

page 65   DNA

page 66   Dos Espirales

page 67   Double Spiral

page 68   Fantasy Nouveau

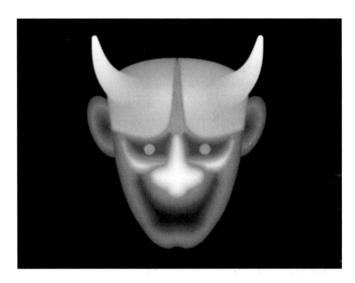

page 69   Han-nya

page 70   Hello

page 71   Hot-Air Balloon

Revelations

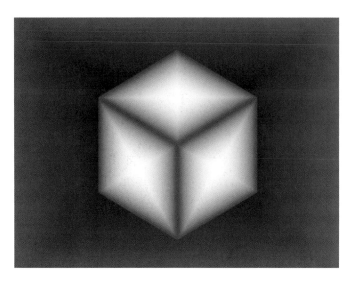

page 72   Indented Cubes

page 73   Inverted Spheres

page 74   Lock & Key

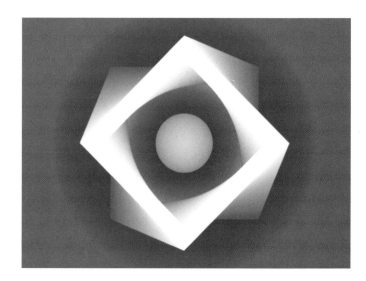

page 75   Mystic Shapes

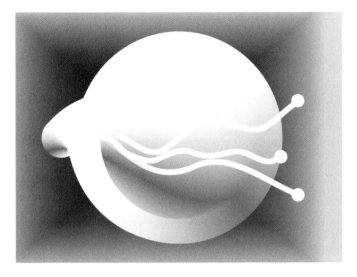

page 76   An Interesting Shape

page 77   Rings

page 78   Entanglements

page 79   Shamrock

Revelations

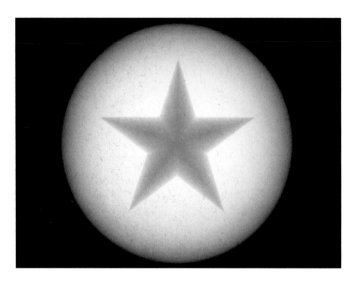

page 80   Star

page 81   Star of David

page 82   Sunflower

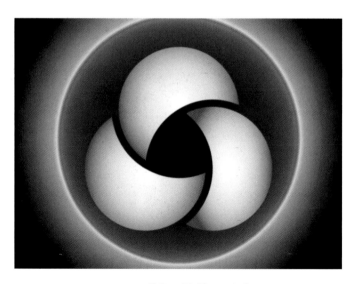

page 83   Trilogy 1

page 84   Trilogy 2

page 85   5 Rings

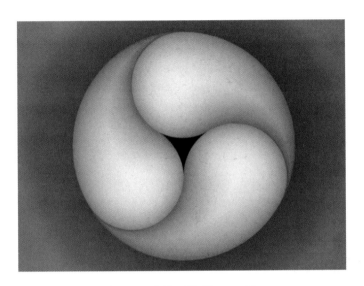

page 86   Anasazi Petroglyphs

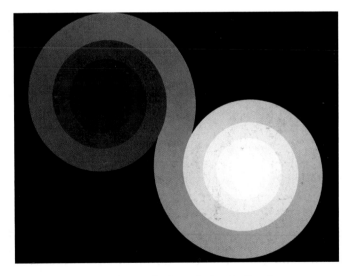

page 87   Artemisia Spirals

Revelations

page 88   Cards

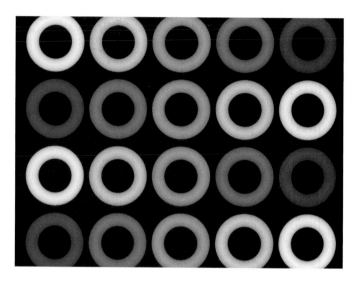

page 89   Circles

page 90   Cube & Hoop

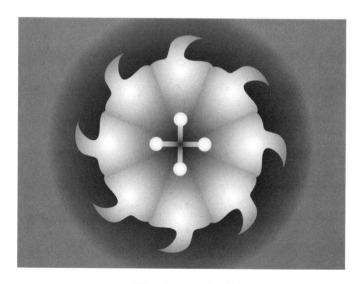

page 91   Desert Flower

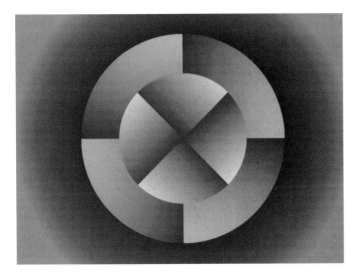

page 92   Equinox

page 93   Floating Cheese Burgers

page 94   Golden Medley

page 95   Grass Cylinder

Revelations

page 96   Hole in my Heart

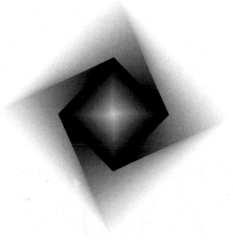

page 97   Hole in the Desert

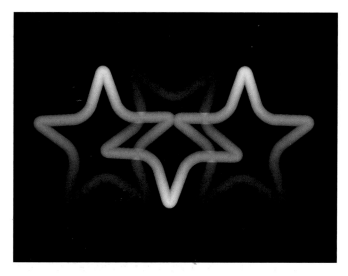

page 98   Interlocking Stars

page 99   The Maze

Revelations

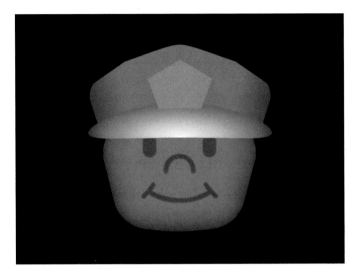

page 100   Officer Winkie

page 101   Opposites Attract

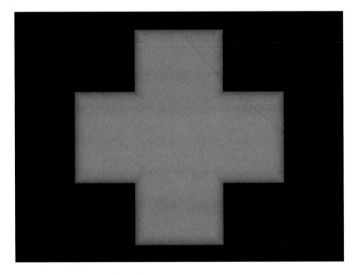

page 102   Pluses

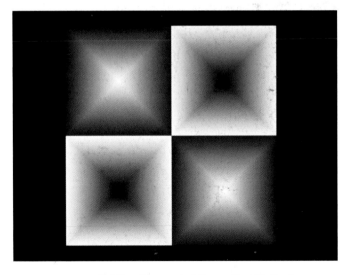

page 103   Pyramids – In & Out

Revelations

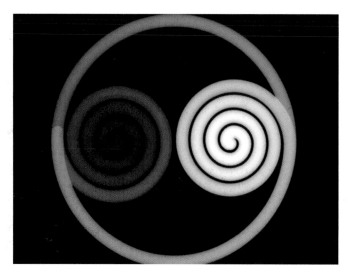

page 104   Spirals – In & Out

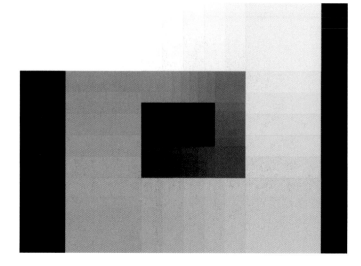

page 105   Square Staircase

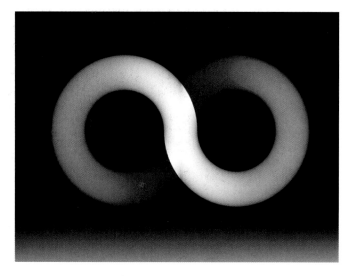

page 106   Infinity 1

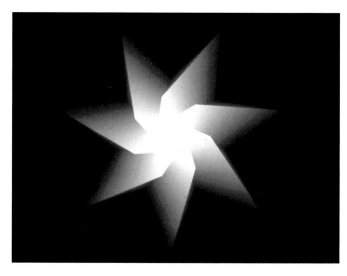

page 107   Twisting Star

page 108   Window

page 109   Words

page 110   Winter Trees

page 111   Leafy Globe

Revelations

page 112   Magic Cube

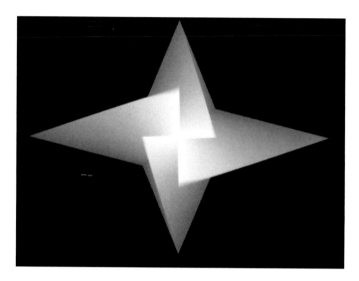

page 113   Marble Star

page 114   Mixed Messages

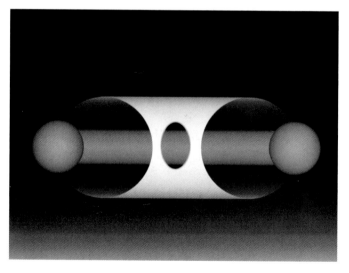

page 115   Mystic Tubes

page 116   Owl

page 117   Pentagon Star

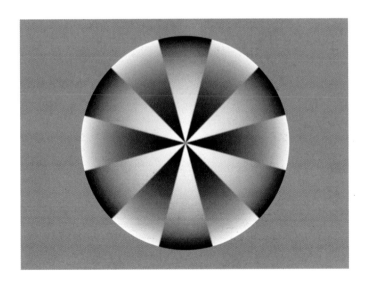

page 118   Pine Wedges

page 119   Planets

Revelations

page 120   Spiral Star

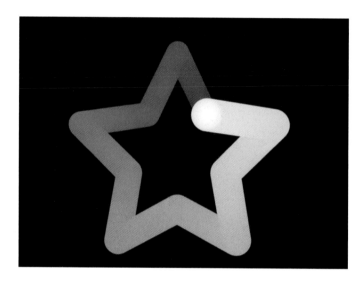

page 121   Rocky Star

page 122   Snow Angel

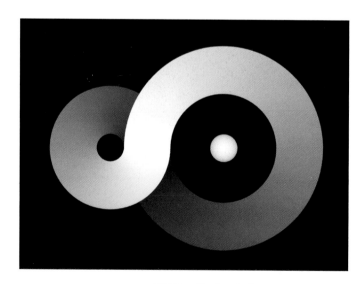

page 123   Spiral 8

Revelations

page 124   Rock Star

page 125   Split Circles

page 126   Piggy

page 127   Stereogram

Revelations

page 128   Susan's Basket

page 129   Teddy Bear

page 130   Vertigo

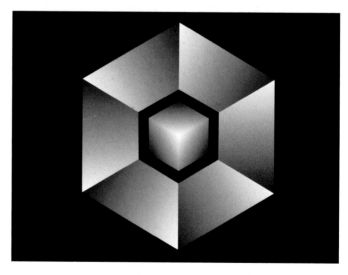

page 131   Windmill

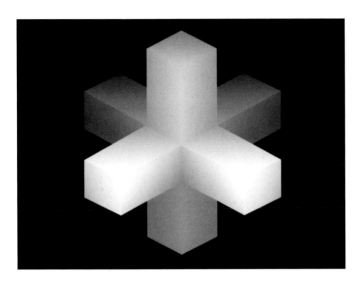

page 132   Cross Plus

page 133   Celtic Knot

page 134   Lizard Bowls

page 135   Morning Glory

Revelations

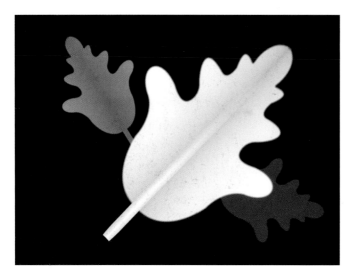

page 136   Oak Leaves

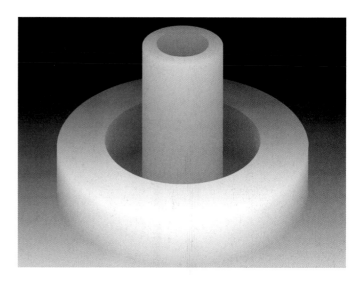

page 137   Pipe & Ring

page 138   Pool Balls

page 139   Stars & Stripes

page 140   New Mexico

page 141   Open the Door

page 142   Organic Vacuum

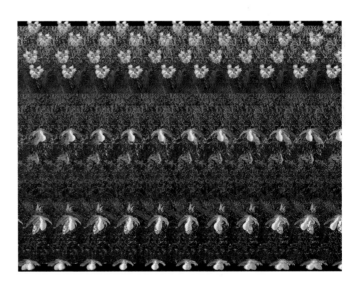

page 143   Orchid Hedge

Revelations

page 144   1 to 10

page 145   Abalone

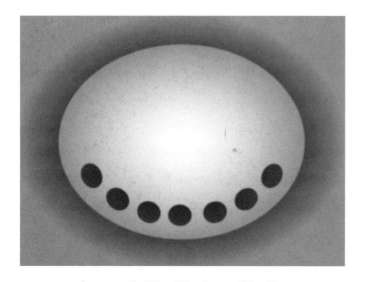

page 146   Abalone Shell

page 147   Amphora

page 148   Banner

page 149   Blue Angel

page 150   Building Blocks

page 151   Celadon

Revelations

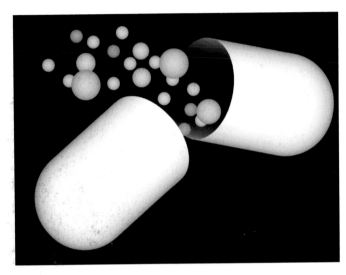

page 152   Chrome Capsule

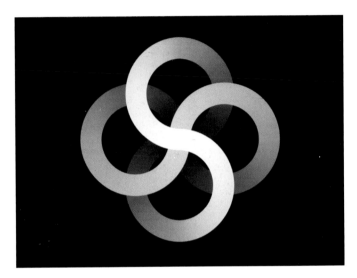

page 153   Clover Leaf

page 154   Dangerous Sea

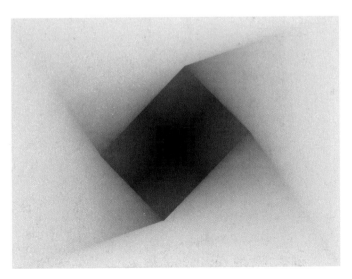

page 155   Deep Hole

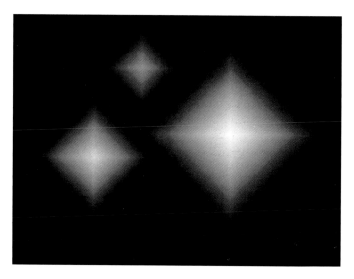

page 156   Desert Pyramid

page 157   Enigma Circles

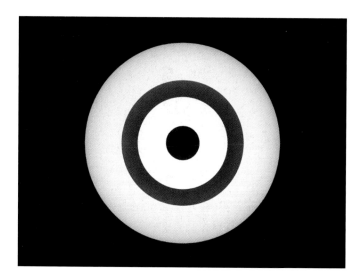

page 158   Eye of the Storm

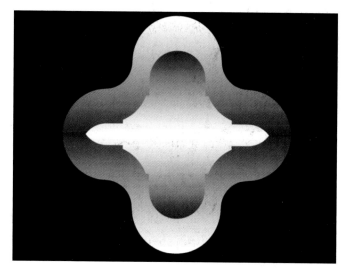

page 159   Flip Flop

Revelations

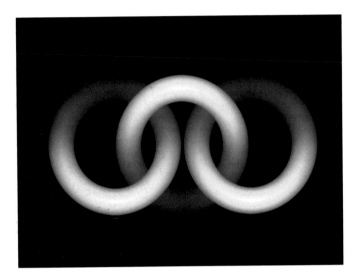

page 160   Interlocking Rings

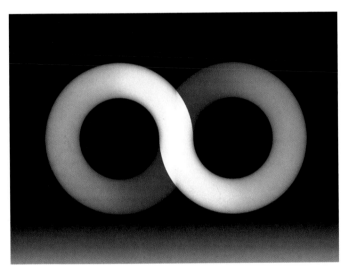

page 161   Infinity 2

page 162   Happy Face

page 163   Infinity 3

page 164   Ivy Cube

page 165   Pound Note

page 166   Stereosaurs

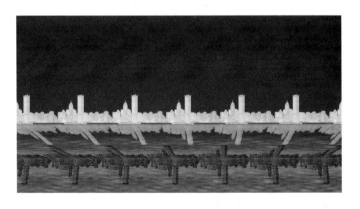

page 167   Reflections of Chicago

Revelations

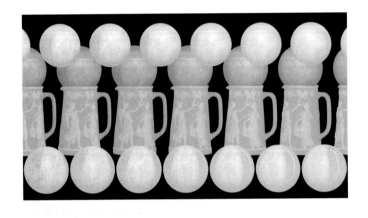

page 168   Wedgwood Blue

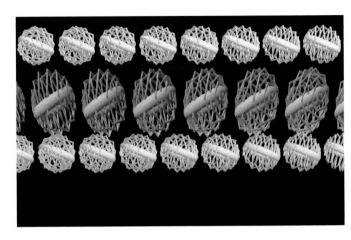

page 169   Torus Cage

page 170   Kaleidoscopic Spiral

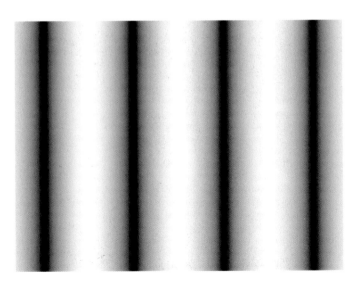

page 171   Chrome Jungle

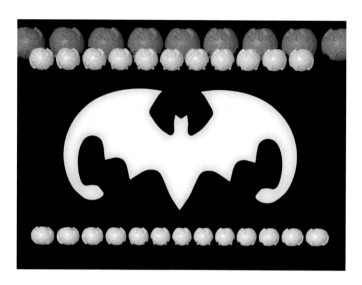

page 172   Granite Fu

page 173   Black Cat in a Coalmine

page 174   French Chow

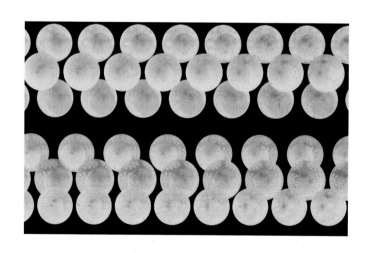

page 175   Enbubbled

Revelations

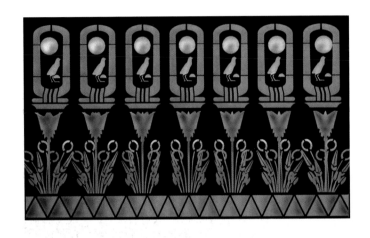

page 176   Sunset on the Nile

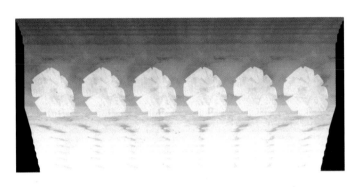

page 177   Rising Sun

page 178   Lucky Rabbit

page 179   Mesa Verde

page 180   Forest Birds

page 181   Two Hearts

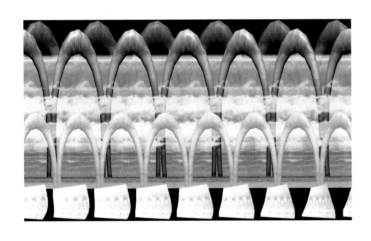

page 182   Sea Palace

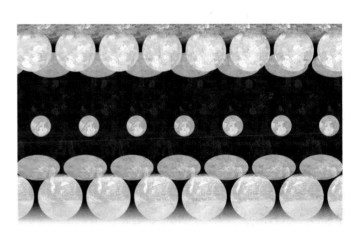

page 183   River Canopy

Revelations

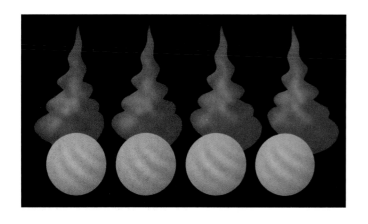

page 184   Inspiration

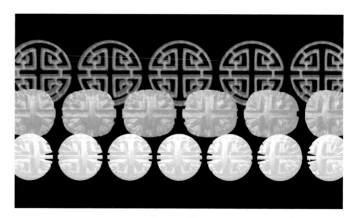

page 185   Jade Riches

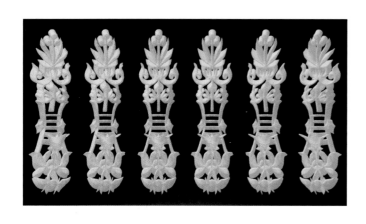

page 186   Lotus Garden

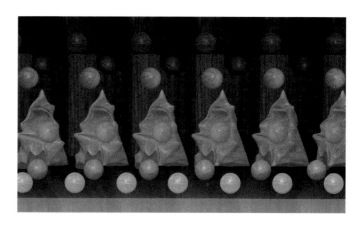

page 187   Koa Construction

Revelations

page 188   Floating Eyes

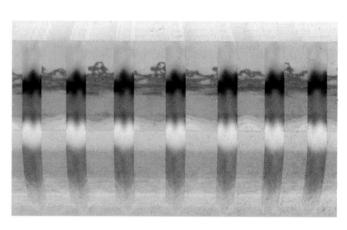

page 189   Palais du Lac

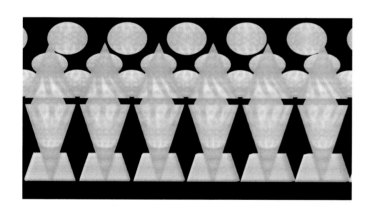

page 190   Byzantine Crystal

page 191   Edge of the Woods

Revelations

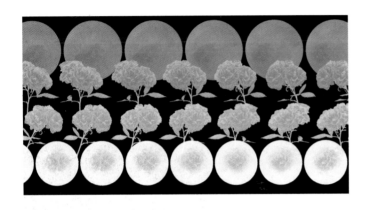

page 192   Rose Rows

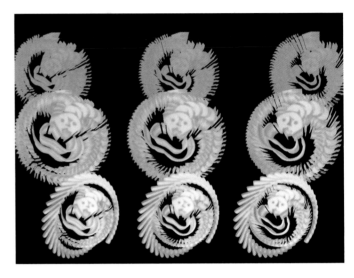

page 193   Scorpions

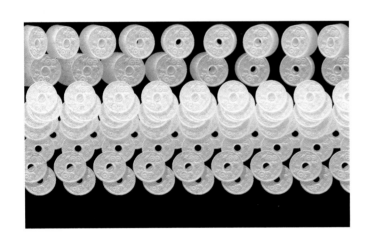

page 194   Four Hundred 50 Yen

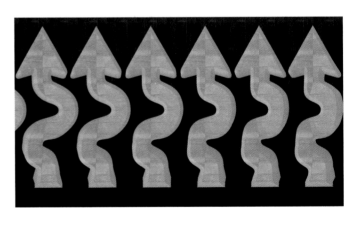

page 195   Straight as an Arrow

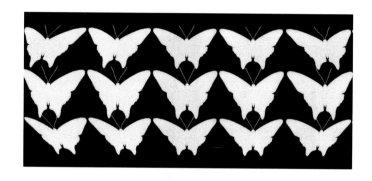

page 196   Blue Butterfly

page 197   Butterfly Lines

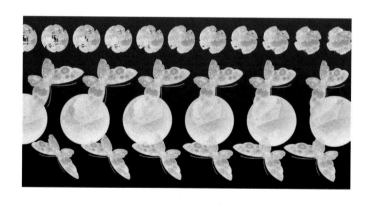

page 198   Butterfly Scarf

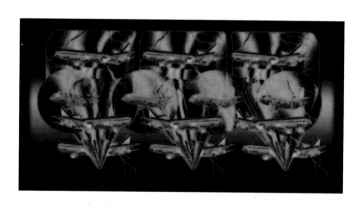

page 199   Holding Pattern

Revelations

page 200   Pyramid Valley

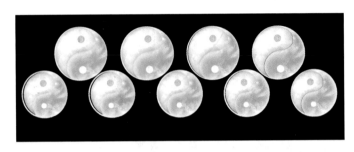

page 201   Yang Yin

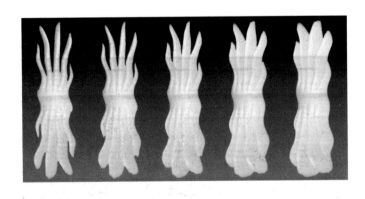

page 202   Swimming Ocean

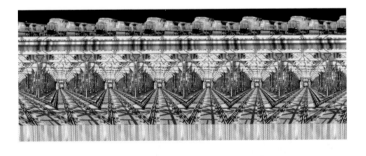

page 203   End of the Line

page 204   Sunset

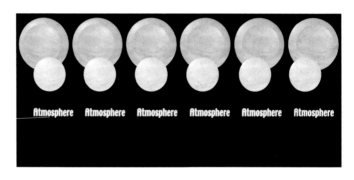

page 205   Atmosphere

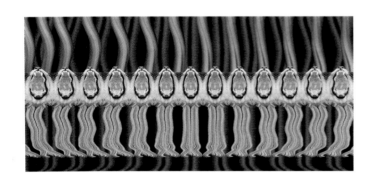

page 206   Uproar

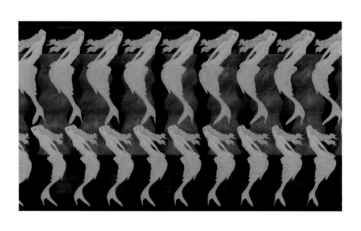

page 207   Mermaid